HAPPINESS in OVERLOOKED MIRACLES

HAPPINESS in OVERLOOKED MIRACLES

Orlando, Fl, USA Sept/2020
Revised in Nov/20201

DR. ENG. FAHIM JAUHARY

HAPPINESS IN OVERLOOKED MIRACLES
ORLANDO, FL, USA SEPT/2020 REVISED IN NOV/20201

iUniverse books may be ordered through booksellers or by contacting:

iUniverse
1663 Liberty Drive
Bloomington, IN 47403
www.iuniverse.com
844-349-9409

Because of the dynamic nature of the Internet, any web addresses or links contained in this book may have changed since publication and may no longer be valid. The views expressed in this work are solely those of the author and do not necessarily reflect the views of the publisher, and the publisher hereby disclaims any responsibility for them.

Any people depicted in stock imagery provided by Getty Images are models, and such images are being used for illustrative purposes only. Certain stock imagery © Getty Images.

ISBN: 978-1-6632-3273-1 (sc)
ISBN: 978-1-6632-3272-4 (e)

Library of Congress Control Number: 2022906826

Print information available on the last page.

iUniverse rev. date: 04/11/2022

A Word of Thanks and Gratitude

When we reach what we dream of, we must remember with a word of thanks those who contributed to our journey and supported us. As the Messenger of God (peace be upon him) has said, "God does not thank those who do not thank people."

So I would like here to express my love and gratitude to my wife, who has always stood by me in the development of this book. She has provided me with her ideas and thoughts about the holy Qur'an.

In addition, I am thankful to my daughters and sons, who have supported me strongly throughout the writing of this book, and have contributed to their opinions and ideas.

I would like to extend my special thanks to my beloved daughter Majd, who lives in New York. She has devoted much time to clarifying English expressions in this second English edition.

Dr. Fahim Jauhary

CONTENTS

INTRODUCTION

When God created this world and subsequently created humans to test them, He inspired in the human happiness and misery, and left the human mind free to choose. The human mind since creation has developed with language, perception, and knowledge about the surrounding world.

God sent messengers to bring gradual knowledge of Islam. Islam is submission to the orders of our Creator and abandonment of what He has prohibited. It is the building of human character, faith, and freedom necessary for self-government and for people to live in happiness.

Since ancient times, God has sent down to every nation many inspired messengers, some of whom we have heard of and some of whom we have not. Their task is to teach humanity Islam and how to live happily as Muslims. God sent Noah, Hood, Saleh, Abraham, Jonah, Moses, and Jesus, among many others. Lastly, God sent Mohammad. Peace be upon them all.

But people distorted and modified the prophets' messages according to their liking. Most prophets were endowed by God with practical and physical miracles to help convince people of their message. As for Prophet Mohammad, his miracle was the holy Qur'an—the last message, preserved without change by its Creator, a book full of linguistic, scientific, and spiritual miracles. From the Qur'an, basic laws can be derived to write into human constitutions in justice and freedom, suitable for every time and place, so that people of all sorts can live happily.

Before the advent of God's message in Mecca, ignorance was widespread in the entire world. Human values were almost nonexistent. Slavery was a common practice among nations. The strong killed the weak. Son-shopping and prostitution were common. Female infanticide was widespread among the poor. Within forty years of the arrival of Prophet Mohammad's message, one of the largest ruling states in history had been built with Islam as its religion. Its borders stretched from the Mediterranean to the Indian peninsula. Empires fell that had dominated the region for thousands of years. The reason is that Prophet Mohammad and his honorable companions, the Sahaba, addressed nations with the words of God. They taught the holy Qur'an in word and deed.

The Sahaba had high intellectual maturity, and they benefited from the wisdom of Prophet Mohammad. In the Qur'an, what is mind purification and intellectual maturity, and what is wisdom?

> God said, "Our lord sends amongst them a
> Messenger of their own, who shall rehearse
> Thy Signs and Wisdom, and sanctify them: for
> you are the exalted in might, the Wise."[1]

The holy Qur'an, which was sent by God for all people, has an influence on the minds of those who contemplate and think. I have witnessed people—from different parts of the world and whose language is not Arabic—either convert to Islam or develop a respect toward Islam once they understand what is

---

[1] Albaqara, verse 129.

written in the Qur'an. Their appreciation of Islam is stronger and deeper than some people who claim to be born Muslim. Islam needs neither preciosity nor sermons and appearances. Islam needs a conscious mind and an honest self. But here I respect and do not deny what many of our distinguished scholars do in clarifying the thoughts of the holy Qur'an, and their dedication to traveling around the world to educate God's servants about the heavenly messages. God preserved the holy Qur'an for the worlds. As He descended upon Prophet Mohammad,

> God said, "We have, without doubt, descended the Message, and we will assuredly guard it."[2]

The Qur'an is an original compilation and the final verbal avowal from God to humankind. The Qur'an is a masterpiece of immense literary value. It is a continuation and a completion of the tasks assigned to the prophets Abraham, Moses, and Jesus. The Qur'an has a wealth of information—both worldly wisdom and intellectual conceptions—that provides the code of life for all humankind.

God said:

> "The Messenger believes in what was revealed to him from his Lord, as do the men of faith. Each one (of them) believes in God, His angels, His Books, and His messengers. We make no distinction (they say) between any of His messengers." And they say, "We hear, and we obey. (We seek) Your forgiveness, our Lord, and

---

[2] Alhijr, verse 9.

to You is the destiny." "God does not burden any soul beyond its capacity. To its credit is what it earns, and against it is what it commits. "Our Lord do not condemn us if we forget or fall into error. Our Lord do not burden us as You have burdened those before us. Our Lord do not lay on us a burden greater than we have strength to bear. Blot out our sins and grant us forgiveness. Have mercy on us. You are our protector; help us against those who stand against faith".[3]

Why do we not address the world with the wisdom facts included in the Qur'an?

It is a mission for those whom God has granted the privilege of wandering in His possession, and God will hold us accountable if we fail to carry this message.

I have written this brief book in the hope that it will be helpful for Muslims and non-Muslims, assisting them to understand the thoughts in the Qur'an as I understand them. The Qur'an contains a huge number of miracles that are overlooked or forgotten, including spiritual miracles that are at the heart of our material lives. I hope the reader can feel the effect of realizing and understanding these miracles as I have felt them in my life.

Current generations believe in the tangible, not in the impalpable or metaphysical. They have no time to delve into the sermons and interpretations of our ancestors. That is why the topics in this book include the importance of maturity and its role in understanding common sense, as well as the importance of knowledge, which leads to wisdom. Maturity,

---

[3] Al Baqarah verses 285, 286.

knowledge, and wisdom are the most important tools for persuading and dealing with people.

I probe the structure of humans, physical and spiritual. I discuss the definitions of faith, belief, will, and desire and their relationship to human habits, building personality and determining destiny. I include my thoughts about the doctrine of reality, the laws of life, the scientific miracles in the Qur'an, and the concepts of slavery and extravagance.

I say, reading a book is thinking about using someone's mind.

The discussions in this book are my personal and diligent subjective efforts; hence, there is the possibility I may be wrong. God is all-knowing. I hope that I have succeeded in what I intended, for my jealousy of human happiness.

Dr. Eng. Fahim N. Jauhary

1

WHO AM I?

When I was in elementary school, my father—God's mercy on him—told me that I should think of myself as a huge palace or a huge building of knowledge. Every day of my life would be a stone in that building. Thus, before sleeping, I should ask myself what new information I had added to the building that day. When the building is complete, I will be happy.

What he was telling me was that I always have to seek knowledge because knowledge gives happiness. My father lost his own father early in life and did not find in his childhood a role model to direct him to knowledge. His colleagues who experienced life with living fathers had great careers and became important figures.

During my early school years, teachers used scare tactics and warned us about hellfire, the torment of the grave, and the like. They described how we would be punished if we made a mistake in reading a verse from the Qur'an, the meaning of which we did not understand at the time. After I finally learned the Qur'an by heart, my family celebrated: a taxi tour around the city, topped by a decorated chair. All of this did not help me get the knowledge of God.

From a young age, I have searched for knowledge— scientific knowledge, psychological knowledge, philosophical knowledge, and theological knowledge. Does God exist?

Where is He? How do we know? I was and still am curious to learn and know how everything works. I did not find answers then. I am certain that knowledge gives us happiness. So I have gone on to read a lot of books and periodicals.

My days passed by. I was an ambitious creature. I finished school and started working to cover my university expenses. After receiving my doctorate in technical engineering, I worked as a researcher and teaching assistant at the university. I focused on reading books about natural sciences, philosophy, psychology, and administration, among other topics, to gain the understanding of different topics and ideologies. I also enjoyed reading the biographies of great people in history. I have sought to find answers to perplexing questions from thinkers who wrote in the German, English, and Arabic languages. I am still curious; I'm trying to learn.

As a result, I am proud that I am now aware of the noble goals of Islam, and I am sure there is a Creator of this universe. Islam came to the whole world with a logical philosophy; it is universal. As Prophet Mohammad said, "There is no virtue for an Arab over a Non-Arab or a white man over a black man except by piety."[4]

For a Muslim, the world is his homeland, and the land of God is wide.

Islam has established rules and laws for this life and the afterlife. These laws of life are made by God, the Creator of life. There are many laws for everything: are we aware of them, and do we think deeply about them?

---

[4] Sahih Al-Bukhari, ISBN-13:978-1567445190, Maktba Dar-US-Islam Al-Albani, page 361.

2

PERCEPTION AND MATURATION

There are two aspects of human maturity: mental maturity and personal maturity. Maturity is the ability to respond to the environment decently. One's thoughts change as one gets older; one's views evolve over time. Maturity stems from one's environment, which provides learning experiences; from the vision or insight granted by God; and from one's awareness, sensory, mental, and scientific.

God says"

> "It is He who has created for you hearing, sight, and hearts (heart's vision): little thanks it is ye give."[5]

Sensory perception or feeling—hearing, vision, and heart insight—is the beginning stage of perception in human beings. It is followed by mental perception, and then scientific perception. If we deny feeling, we deny perception and deny maturation! The Almighty says about false believers:

---

[5] Al-Mo'menoon, verse 78

"Fain, they deceive Allah and those who believe, but they only deceive themselves, and realize it not."[6]

God also says,

"Truly it is not their eyes that are blind, but their hearts which are in their breasts."[7]

This means that God abolished the initial sense of insight, causing the loss of mental and scientific awareness of God's existence.

That concept appears clearly in the following Quranic verses:

"Nay, man will be insight against himself, even though he was to put up his excuses."[8]

"Now, Insights (Proofs) have come to you, from your Lord, if any will see, it will be for his own soul, if any will be blind, it will be to his own (harm)."[9]

Perception is from clairvoyance or insight. It is the beginning of change for the better. It is the beginning of growth and development. Without clairvoyance, man would live in a loss like animals.

---

[6] Albakara, verse 9.

[7] Alhaj, verse 46.

[8] Alqiama, verse 14, 15.

[9] Alana'am, verse 104.

It is natural for the conscious mind to connect with the different senses and to realize what it lacks in science and knowledge. This is where the function of the unconscious mind comes in. The unconscious mind stores the outcome of perception to be used when needed. This is followed by the role of maturity.

Maturity is the completion of experience and wisdom in matters of life. Maturity is the ability to distinguish between what is right and what is wrong, between what is good and what is evil, between what benefits you and what does not benefit you, between what it means to live happily and what it means to live wretchedly. Maturity is not granted at birth. Maturity gives a person the concept of life and the ability to think about various issues.

A person's growth is considered the first and most indispensable stage of maturity. Nevertheless, intellectual maturity is not related to age. The age of a mature person is just a number. Maturity is an endless intellectual station.

We can group signs of a person's maturity into five categories.

Dealing with Thoughts

Happiness is dependent on one's thoughts. So change depends on one's way of thinking, not on altering one's environment or being promoted at work. A mature man does not get excited by calamities or charity. He does not believe all that is said. Rather, he examines information to see what is behind it and questions its validity before accepting it.

Dealing with the Self

Happiness is in self-evaluation and not comparison to others. A mature man respects himself, assumes responsibility for his actions, admits his mistakes, and works to change. In contrast, the immature person always complains and blames circumstances or others for his lack of success. A mature man knows himself, his capabilities, and what he wants in life. Therefore, he builds his future within the limits of his capabilities and does not wait for coincidences. He begins by understanding the small things before he talks about the big ones. He does not let others' judgment of him affect his life. He loves knowledge and reading.

Dealing with the Creator

A mature man depends on his Creator. He is pure in heart and honest. He loves people. A mature man tries to stay optimistic and satisfied with what God has destined for him. He gives because he wants to, not to seek gratitude from anyone.

Dealing with People

Humans are not angels. Do not gossip. A mature man forgives. He repays harm with good deeds. God said,

> "Repel (Evil) with what is better. Then will he between whom and thee was hatred become as it were thy friend and intimate."[10]

---

[10] Fussilat, verse 34.

7

A mature man knows when to speak and when to be silent. He understands the causes of others' behavior toward him. He maintains good relations and learns to withdraw from harmful relationships. He leaves arguments even if he is sure of his opinions. He is happy to talk to strangers and to learn new ideas and concepts.

Dealing with the Environment and the Outside World

Adapting to circumstances is one of the most important foundations of happiness. A mature man adapts quickly to a changing, non-ideal world to find the best in everything. He lets go of the past and takes the present. He is aware of the real value of things and does not get deceived by advertisements and brands. He loves to travel and enjoys life without caution. He enjoys increasing his knowledge of the world and people.

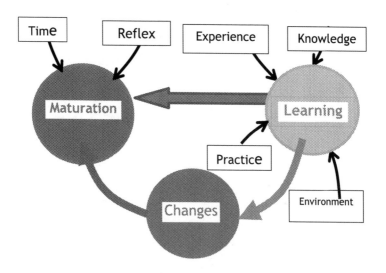

3

WISDOM

The word "wisdom" can be defined as the "integration of deep understanding, knowledge, and experience, which includes tolerance toward uncertainty in life."[11] Wisdom is an important element of the human personality and encompasses many characteristics, including experience, knowledge, and intelligence. Some have also defined wisdom as the science in which we seek the truth. Wisdom is realizing the right thing to say and the right way to act through healthy mental reasoning. It can also mean possessing a clear insight into many issues. The virtue of wisdom is in the holy Qur'an. Almighty said,

"He grant wisdom to whom He please; and he to whom wisdom is granted receive indeed a benefit overflowing, but none will grasp the Message but men of understanding."[12]

Prophet Mohammad said", "There is no envy except in two: a man whom God gave him money, as he uses it on the right,

---

[11] Stephen S. Hall, From Philosophy to Neuroscience, Book, Amazon.

[12] Albaqara 269.

9

and a man who God gave him wisdom, as he judges with it and teaches it."[13]

Our prophet Jesus Christos (poh) said", "Wisdom is the light of every heart."[14]

Scholars"[15] have studied the concept of wisdom since ancient times. In 450 BC, the Greek thinker and philosopher Aristotle said, "Wisdom is the head of science, literature, and art; it is the inoculation of understanding and the results of minds." [16]

As his classical mathematics teacher, Plato said, the four virtues are wisdom, justice, courage, and moderation.

Socrates, the wise teacher of Plato and the founder of Western philosophy, said much more:

Diseases without medicine: lack of religion and lack of literature.

No virtue without knowledge.

Minds of talents and science gains.

Who is stingy on himself is less to the others.

Great woman is the one who teaches us how to love.

Socrates was asked: Why have you been chosen to be the wisest of the wise men in Greece?

He replied: Maybe because I'm the only man who admits he doesn't know."[17]

---

[13] Sahih Al-Bukhari, ISBN-13:978-1567445190, Maktba Dar-US-Islam.

[14] Bihar Al-Anwar, V.14, P.317,No 17.

[15] Bertrand Russell, The history of western Philosophy, Book published by Simon & Schuster, NY.

[16] S.Ryan, Wisdom, Stanford Encyclopedia of Philosophy/Spring 2007 ed.

[17] The Trials of Socrates, famous-trials.com.

The German philosopher Jog Wilhelm Hegel"[18] defined wisdom as the highest possible level of man. After knowledge is complete and history reaches its peak, then wisdom is born in man. Wisdom is the next and last stage of philosophy; it is the climax and the end. Congratulations to those who reach wisdom and sobriety.

Wisdom gives man great moral character and a sense of balance. It generates awareness of how events can be handled. Wisdom requires several qualities, such as calmness and poise at a time of calamity. It is essential in various matters of life, good and bad. It leads to looking at things on a deeper level to find the root causes of problems and to reach the best possible solutions.

Wisdom is one of the attributes of prophets, apostles, and the righteous. God said to Prophet Mohammad", "And you are of a great moral character."[19]

Wisdom is one of the qualities of those scientists who ponder the creation of heaven and earth. Wisdom helps man be more accurate in his words and actions, which elevates his status among others. With wisdom, a human mind becomes looked up to by those around him, who enjoy hearing his thoughts and opinions.

So who is a wise person? "Al-Hakim" in Arabic means a reasonable person who is likely to steer decisions toward righteousness due to his life experience. Yet it is not a certainty that someone with a large amount of life experience will be wise. One of the qualities of Al-Hakim is that he is always optimistic about his ability to solve most of life problems. He

---

[18] Stephen S. Hall, From Philosophy to Neuroscience, Book, Amazon.
[19] Al-Qalam, verse 4.

has a positive outlook in the darkest situations. He is calm and careful when faced with difficult decisions. He uses his sense and intelligence to draw important points from different perspectives. The psychologist Igor Grossman"[20] says that wisdom is associated with positive effects on human life, which reduces his negative feelings. He also said that "a wise person has a relatively long life and has good social relationships."

A wise person is characterized by a set of qualities[21], including the following:

- the ability to analyze and draw lessons from knowledge and experiences in his field of specialization; age is not a factor but maturity is essential
- the ability to be honest, neutral in judgment, and unmoved by desires, vanity, and self-love
- the ability to look at things positively and realistically, even in self-critique.
- the ability to think quietly before speaking, since words that comes out of the mouth cannot be unspoken
- the ability to understand others and work like an investigator, without judging bad or good, to give the best advice
- the ability to accept others as they are without changing their actions.

To be wise in your opinions, you must investigate all of your life experiences to extract the wisdom, causes, and results.

---

[20] Igor Grossman, Wisdom Bias & Balance, Journal Article 2018 Dec., Waterloo Univ.Canada.

[21] Adam Grant, How to think like a wise Person, Syndicated from linkedin, Nov 20, 2013.

You should look at your life experiences in social, emotional, scientific, and cognitive contexts to turn your experiences into pearls of wisdom. Everything we go through is not a coincidence or luck. It is destined for you from within or outside your will. If you understand this, you will advance your mind and grasp different concepts. You will be able to give out the right judgment.

Wisdom is the juice of life experiences. It is a wealth of all kinds of accidents and anecdotes. You will be convinced that your life experiences have informed your conscious understanding of everything that surrounds you.

4

HUMAN STATE

The human being at any time and place is a standing state, like any country of this world. It has its eras, changing places, and multiple climates. God created the human being from seven elements: **mind, self, character, body, spirit, clairvoyance** (insight), and **instinct** (common sense). Then God ordered humans to use their minds in judgment according to their time and place, in a way that does not contradict with what is imposed upon them in established laws of justice, freedom, and worship. God imposed on man to enjoy good and forbid wrong, as these are recognized in one's era, for the continuity of a decent and happy life.

The human being, then, is a sovereign state. The **Self** dwells in the **Body** and then experiences death and exits it. The Almighty said,

> "And if you could see how wicked are in the dark of death, and the angels stretch forth their hands, saying: yield up yourselves out today."[22]

The **Self** in the body is the ruler. In the human body, the self is governed by the physical laws of the body. The mind is the general manager, while the body parts can be looked at

---

[22] Alan'am, verse 93.

as the people. The constitution of this state is the character, which is politicized by the self. The character controls the mind, and the mind in turn orders body parts such as the hand, eye, and tongue to move. These tools have no right to rebel against the mind. Some minds are kind to the body because they are aware of the shared common interests. But other minds do not consider what will happen to the body. These minds are ruled by foolish and faulty personalities. As for the involuntary movements of the body such as circulation, breathing, and appetite, they are controlled by instinct.

The puzzling question here is Do other creatures, such as birds and animals, have the self?

God said,

"There is not an animal that lives on neither the earth, nor a being that fly with its wings, but nations like you. Nothing has We omitted from the Book, and they all shall be gathered to their Lord in the end."[23]

From this verse we can conclude that creatures return to their Lord after death, on the day of resurrection. In my humble opinion, this means that they have selves in their bodies, but are not held accountable because God did not give them freedom of will. And if they have selves, then they have character or personality that serves as a fixed constitution for their lives. But God knows better.

To control the body, first, we refine our Character: wisdom, love of others, goodness, forgiveness, and sincerity at work.

---

[23] Al-Anam, verse 38.

These are all good qualities of character that create a good, happy life.

False pride, enmity, hatefulness, hatred, foolishness, envy, cunning, and laziness are qualities of bad character. They destroy life and create unhappiness for a man and those around him.

God said,

> "Nor can goodness and Evil be equal, repel (Evil) with what is better. Then will he between whom and thee was hatred become as it were thy friend and intimate. And no one is granted such goodness except those who exercise patience and self-restraint, none but persons of the greatest good fortune."[24]

These verses urge us to forgive and to be patient in distress. God said,

> "So that ye may not despair over matters that, neither pass you by, nor exult over favors bestowed upon you. For Allah loveth not any vainglorious boaster."[25]

This verse calls on man to rely on God and be patient with what has happened to him. It warns us against false pride.

---

[24] Fusilat, verses 34–35.
[25] Alhaded, verse 23.

God said,

"And from the mischief of the envious one as he practices envy."[26]

Envy is an evil that has an impact on the envious, but God protects the believer from envy.

God said,

"Satan plans is to excite enmity and hatred between you, with intoxicants and gambling, and hinder you from the remembrance of Allah, and from prayer: will ye not then abstain?"[27]

In this verse, God forbids drinking and gambling because they poison the character, which is responsible for controlling the mind and can cause hostility and hatred among us.

---

[26] Alfalak, verse 5.
[27] Almaida, 91.

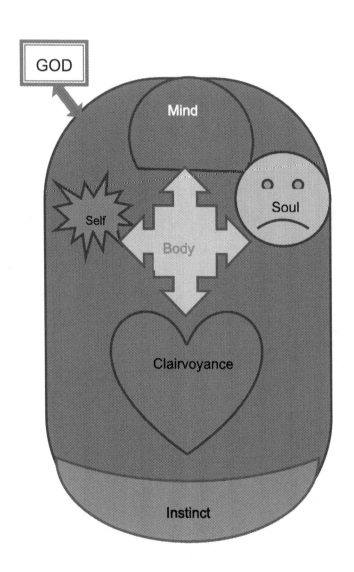

5

SOUL AND INSTINCT

As I mentioned earlier, the human entity consists of seven elements: **mind, self, character, body, spirit, clairvoyance** (insight), and **instinct** (common sense). The spirit belongs to the domain and knowledge of God, and humans were given a small part of it. It has been proven from the holy Qur'an that God breathed into man from his soul.

God said,

> "They ask you concerning the Spirit, say: 'The Spirit by command of my Lord of knowledge, it is only a little that is communicated to you. If it were Our Will, We could take away that which We have sent you by inspiration, then wouldst you find none to plead thy affair in that matter as against Us."[28]

The **Spirit** is from the world of God's command, which does not belong to any time or place. At various points in the holy Qur'an, there are suggestions about the spirit's link with God Almighty. **The implication is that the spirit has nothing**

---

[28] Alisra', verses 85–86.

to do with the self"[29]. Neither history nor modern science has been able to understand the essence of the spirit.

God Almighty created our master Adam from clay and made Adam a living human being with working organs. In a fetus, if fetal growth is complete, God breathes into him from his soul. Then God creates his instinct and clairvoyance. God always supports those who believe in him with his spirit. The breath of God's spirit may be a support or a connection between God Almighty and man. The Qur'an is a spirit inspired by God in his prophet. Accordingly, **spirit might not be life; instead, it is a connection to God.**

God knows better. God said,

> "You will not find any people who believe in Allah and His Messenger, even though... for such, He has written Faith in their hearts, and strengthened them with a Spirit from Himself."[30]

When a man dies, his **Soul** leaves his body, and the knowledge in his mind fades. As for the **Self**, it goes back to her Creator in the isthmus. The **Body** decomposes into methane, ethane, phosphine, and so on. These gases oxidize or ignite as soon as they meet the oxygen in the air. If a person drowns in the sea and is eaten by fish, the body turns into a hydrocarbon food for fish.

God knows best.

I may ask, "If we read a message, then words and names enter my mind. But what did our minds absorb? Is it the ink? Is

---

[29] Adnan Al-Rifai, The Great Miracle, Wikipedia.

[30] Almujadala, verse 22.

it the paper? And where does the meaning settle? Is it In my brain?, In my heart? Or Elsewhere?" Dr. Muhammad Shahrour"[31] has stated that God Almighty has all the words and knowledge of everything. What is given to us, whether believers or nonbelievers, as spirit is a very small part of knowledge. The more a person advances in scientific research, the more his spirit increases its knowledge. Yet he will never reach the perfection or the knowledge that exists in his Creator, the one who knows everything. No matter how many discoveries, advances, and inventions humans make, perfect knowledge will never be achieved. If he wishes, God can erase all the knowledge that has been revealed to us.

God has gifted a part of His spirit only to man. He has not given it to other creatures. Man is the creature with **Clairvoyance** and awareness. When a man dies, his soul fades away, and accordingly science fades from his brain.

God knows best.

God taught Adam the names of all things. God has taught us and continues to teach us parts of His knowledge. God taught us the languages, speaking, chemistry, physics, arithmetic, and many other fields of knowledge. He is God, who knows everything.

An animal has no Spirit or **Clairvoyance**; otherwise, a donkey would have been able to create a car. But God gave all creatures, including man, Self and the Instinct to multiply and grow.

God knows best.

Clairvoyance is the power of perception and acumen. God gave humans the ability to express our thoughts verbally

---

[31] Mohammad Shahroor, Book, the Qur'an & the Book, Amazon.

and in writing. Clairvoyance is knowledge and experience obtained through thinking, not imitation—a capacity not found in animals. For example, with his vision, a **human can watch, think, work, develop, express, and argue his opinion in clear and well-developed language,** which is an impossible task for an animal. Therefore, man has been able to develop his life and adapt nature to serve him, while animals remain stagnant, as they were created thousands of years ago. Clairvoyance is perhaps located in the heart of man. God said,

> "Do they not travel through the land, so that their hearts may thus learn wisdom and their ears may thus learn to hear? Truly it is not their eyes that are blind, but their hearts which are in their breasts."[32]

God said also,

> "Nay, man will be evidence against himself."[33]
> ("Evidence" here means sharpness of insight, or clairvoyance.)

I think that the **Self**, it is not from the physical world. It may be a type of energy from another dimension, which science is still trying to understand.

Apparently, soul has been proven to have some physical weight, according to an experiment in which the subject lost

---

[32] Hajj, verse 46.
[33] Alqyama, verse 14.

twenty-two grams of weight immediately after death"[34]. It has also been reported that some patients who underwent periods of zero brain activity during surgery (which is the medical definition of death) have had an out-of-body experience. They were fully aware of their surroundings and were able to look down and watch the doctors try to resuscitate them.

The laws of material life do not apply to the self. When we sleep, we do not feel time. God said,

"It is Allah that takes the self at death, and those that did not die during their sleep those on whom He has passed the decree of death, He keeps back."[35]

God also said,

"And their selves may perish in their very denial of Allah"[36] "Perish" means "die."

As the self gets out of the body, it proceeds to another world, but the soul fades or returns to its divine source.

God reassures the self,

"O that Self, in complete rest and satisfaction, Come back thou to thy Lord, well pleased, and well-pleasing into Him"[37]

---

[34] Duncan MacDougall, Scientific Study published in 1907, Massachusetts.

[35] Alzumar, verse 42.

[36] Altaobah, verse 55.

[37] Alfajr, verses 27–28.

God swears,

> "I do call to witness the Resurrection Day, and I do call to witness the reproaching Self, does the man think we will not gather his bones?"[38]

God said, in the words of our prophet Joseph,

> "Nor do I absolve my Self of blame; the Self is certainly prone to evil."[39]

God created the self of human beings before the body. God said,

> "It is We who created you, then gave you shape, then We bade the angels prostrate to Adam, and they prostrate, not so Iblis, He refused to be of those who prostrate."[40]

From the foregoing, we conclude that there are levels of self-esteem:

- *Reassuring Self*: This is the satisfied self. It is the higher degree of the reproachful self. One has gone beyond the stage of blame, belief in the hereafter, and doomsday thinking. One is merciful, not afraid of death or the torment of the hereafter, because within is the conviction that one has satisfied the Creator. One hopes for His mercy and love. One sees guidance in

---

[38] Alqyamah, verses 1–2.

[39] Yosef, verse 53.

[40] Alaa'raf, verse 11.

the holy Qur'an and thinks about God's miracles and grace.

- *Allaoama (Reproachful) Self*: This is the self who sometimes fails to obey God. One blames oneself. One believes in the hereafter and the day of resurrection. One loves life and may be merciful, but one is afraid of death and the torment beyond the grave. One always fears God and hopes for His mercy.
- *Heretic Self*: This is the self that disbelieves in the hereafter and the Day of Judgment. One says there is nothing after this world, or one is not interested in knowing the Creator and His provisions. One believes in one's own ability to understand life. One lives on anyway, empty and without principles. One may be merciful, but one is afraid to die because one will lose the life one loves.

The human brain is a living organ if the Self is present in it. Other creatures also have brains with self, but not spirit or soul. Animals are sovereign as we are, but we do not feel it.

I believe that, in a certain area of a creature's brain or body, there is an analytical site—what we call the instinct or common sense—with specialized intelligence. It is character or **Conscience**, from which good or evil traits are produced. The type of behavior depends on the genetic instinct of the creature. This analytical site is located somewhere in the bodies of all created things, **whether an animal, a plant, a crystal, or even an atom**. It is the reason for the analytical behavior or specific automatic intelligence of all creatures. Spirit has nothing to do with that.

Animals, such as dogs, fish, and birds, don't do much thinking. They concern themselves with the everyday business of gathering food, drinking, resting, reproducing, and defending themselves. Therefore, their brains are organized around major centers that control these functions.

Many animal species show grief, friendship, gratitude, wonder, and a range of other emotions"[41]. Many animals are very intelligent and have sensory and motor abilities that dwarf ours. Dogs can detect diseases. Elephants, whales, and alligators use low-frequency sounds to communicate over long distances, often miles. Bats, dolphins, whales, frogs, and various rodents use high-frequency sounds to find food, communicate with others, and navigate. Many animals also display wide-ranging emotions, including joy, happiness, empathy, compassion, grief, and even resentment and embarrassment.

Crows, dogs, and lions all have a percentage of analytical intelligence. Plants adapt to the direction of light and the environment; some go even further and intelligently hunt insects.

Birds and some fish and animals migrate thousands of miles and return to their starting point because God has created a sense of place and a sense of direction in their instincts. There is no such instinct in man. If a human is lost in a forest, that human cannot find home without a compass.

The ratio and type of this instinct or this spontaneous intelligence vary from creature to creature. Of course, the human being is special and has the highest percentage, because the human body demands a lot. Humans were created on the earth to build it. A human should be God's successor on

---

[41] Marc Bekoff, Animal Instincts, Berkeley, edu./Mar 08,2011

the earth. Animals and plants are instinctively intelligent only to maintain the species.

We also observe instinctive intelligence in bacteria, fungi, viruses, and even crystals. The crystallization of table salt is cube-shaped. The crystallization of sugar is in the shape of a monocline. The crystallization of silicon is hexagonal. No matter where these materials are—whether in America or Asia or elsewhere—each of their crystals has specific, instinctive qualities that interact with light, magnets, and electricity with specific intelligence.

All creatures behave according to their instincts or common sense, which was created by God in their composition because they were afraid of free will—except for man. Man asked his Lord to allow him free will. Man was unjustly ignorant; he wanted to have his will instinctively free to do what he liked.

God said,

"We did indeed offer the Trust to the Heavens and the Earth and the mountains; but they refused to undertake it; being afraid thereof: but man undertook it, he was indeed unjust and foolish."[42]

We carry free will as chromosomes (RNA) from the cells of our father Adam, long before we were born into this world.

In a more general sense, we can say that instinct creates a healthy fitness by which a creature deals with the environment. It is a creature's cognitive sense that helps it cope with circumstances. God placed instinct in creatures at the birth of

---

[42] Alahzab, verse 72.

each species so that it is consistent within the entire species, without deviation.

Prophet Mohammad said", "Every child is born on Fitrah (instinct), also the beast produces a whole beast, and do you feel it is out of shape?"[43]

---

[43] Sahih Al-Bukhari, ISBN-13:978-1567445190, Maktba Dar-US-Islam

6

KNOWLEDGE-SEEKING IS AN OBLIGATION

Seeking science, knowledge, and meditation on this universe is an obligation placed by God on every human being. God has honored man over all creatures by blowing man out of His soul, creating clairvoyance, making man sane, and making man His successor on the earth.

Science and work are the foundations of civilization, progress, happiness, and the strength of nations. Many Quranic verses and hadiths honor science, scholars, and workers. God said,

> "Those truly fear God, among His Servants, who **have knowledge,** for God is exalted in Might, Oft-Forgiving."[44]

Knowledgeable people realize that there is a Creator. God said,

> "There is no God but He: that is the witness of God, His angels, and those endued with **knowledge**, standing firm on justice."[45]

---

[44] Fater, verse 28.

[45] Al Emran, verse 18.

The knowledgeable are not the same as others. God said,

"Say; 'Are those equal, those who **know** and those who do not know? It is those who are endued with understanding that receives admonition.'"[46]

God urges us to work;

"And say: **work**, soon will God observe your work, and His messenger, and the believers."[47]

In surah Ta'Ha', verse 114, the Creator commands Prophet Mohammad, "And speak; Oh, my Lord, increase my knowledge."

Prophet Mohammad (pbuh) said", "The scholar is preferred over worshiper as my virtue over your lowest."[48] He said" also, "Knowledge seeking is obligatory for every Muslim."[49]

So what is knowledge, and what kind of knowledge is science?

Science and knowledge do not come from the man. They are from God, who gives them to man if man seeks them, whether he is a believer or not. The Creator has placed in His creation of man the attributes of clairvoyance, thought, meditation, and learning. Science is, no doubt, of immemorial origin. Knowledge has accumulated and continues to accumulate. Knowledge is a seed implanted by God, who is knowledgeable about everything.

---

[46] Alzumar, verse 9.
[47] Altaubah, verse 105.
[48] Sahih Al-Bukhari, ISBN-13:978-1567445190, Maktba Dar-US-Islam
[49] Binbaz.org.sa/fatwas

The whole Qur'an is concentrated knowledge of sciences, ethics, history, and more. We are aware every day of scientific discoveries, such as gravity, magnetism, the rotation of the earth, the expansion of the universe, the shrinking of earth's land area, the evolution of human nature inside one's mother's womb, and many more. These are only details of the verses of the holy Qur'an, which is in our hands. In other words, if we think about many verses of the Qur'an in-depth and scientifically, the Qur'an will lead us to an understanding of many scientific facts. As we become aware, recognize truth, and seek truth through science and hard work, many facts about this universe will emerge.

Knowledge, as defined by Sheikh Mitwalli al-Sha'rawi"[50], may God have mercy on him, is twofold:

1 - the science of religion and its branches.

2 - the science of the universe and its branches. The science of the universe includes the inanimate realm (sun, moon, physics, etc.), the plant realm (fixed and living), the animal realm (moving and living), the human realm (such as medicine,) and the work realm.

Cosmologists have, practically in their hands, millions of signs and miracles. If they were successful, intelligent, and bright, they would be inspired to believe in God.

Many people have been guided by scientific facts and found the miracles of the holy Qur'an. Among the examples are the French scientist Maurice Boccia; Isaac Newton, who

---

[50] Mitwalli Sha'rawi, Celestical science & Cosmic science, YouTube.

believed in a monotheistic God; Quillaia and Stanley of Britain; and many others who were Muslim or who acknowledged the greatness of the message prophet, Mohammad.

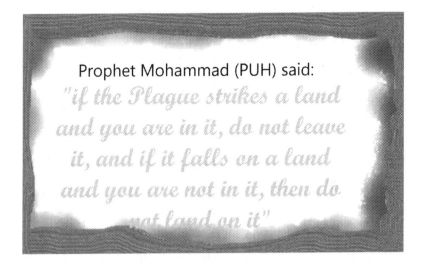

Prophet Mohammad (PUH) said:
"if the Plague strikes a land and you are in it, do not leave it, and if it falls on a land and you are not in it, then do not land on it"

33

7

KNOWLEDGE, FAITH, AND BELIEF

Faith and **belief** are the paradigms of the heart's acceptance of a truth. This **truth does not fall under human senses**. Perhaps it is rejected by your conscious mind and your five senses. Examples of such truths include believing in God and paradise, the greatness of this country, or your capabilities to perform a task. Faith is a way of thinking—a stance of the mind. It is an internal certainty that what you are thinking is perfectly acceptable and clear in your conscious mind and will be embodied within your unconscious mind.

Faith performs miracles, whether it is a faith in the factual or in a myth.

Believing in something without knowledge, reason, or guidance is a force that can sometimes destroy our lives. It can be an **obstacle to our happiness** or **reasons for our happiness**. Therefore, it is preferable that our beliefs be based on facts.

God said,

> "They say: nay! We shall follow the ways of our fathers. What even though their fathers were void of wisdom and guidance."[51]

---

[51] Albaqara, verse 170.

Why do we take in and believe in certain things that are unproven and untested, that have simply been received as habits for hundreds of years? It is necessary for an intelligent human being to reexamine ideas and test them based on new data, the development of our knowledge, and the development of our minds. To know what benefits us and what harms us in the reality of our affairs is compatible with the constants of faith in our religion.

The Qur'an is filled with science and guidance. The words "**science**" and "**knowledgeable**" are mentioned in many verses. God distinguishes those who are knowledgeable from those who are not knowledgeable. Those who are not knowledgeable believe in things according to customs and traditions, without using thought.

Knowledge is not restricted to the constants of religion. It includes nature, morals, and that entire creation of God in this world. Science is the foundation of civilizations; it is the progress and power of man. Because of this, many verses and hadiths honor science and scientists.

In surah Jonah verse 5, God narrate scientific information. He says,

> "It is He who made the sun radiant, and the moon a light, and determined phases for it—that you may know the number of years and the calculation. God did not create all this without truth. He details the revelations for people who know"[52].

---

[52] Jonah, verse 5

It has been said that science is light and ignorance is darkness. It has also been said that ignorance is revenge and science is mercy.

Confucius said"[53], "The man who asks a question is a fool for a minute, the man who does not ask is a fool for life."

Philip K. Dick said"[54], "Reality is that which, when you stop believing in it, doesn't go away."

Seeking knowledge in Islam is considered obligatory. One must seek not only knowledge of nature, religion, and medicine, but also the knowledge of all we do. We must know their validity and compatibility with the curriculum laid down for us by the Creator.

Ralph W. Emerson said"[55], "All I have seen teaches me to trust the Creator for all I have not seen."

Simply, knowledge gives us pleasure. If I make myself a cup of coffee, I'm going to drink it with pleasure, because I know what's in it and how I made it.

Ali Bin Abu-Talib said"[56], "Win knowledge, you live forever. Then unknowledgeable people are dead, but that of knowledge are alive."

---

[53] Confucius, Famous Quotes About life, Amazon.

[54] Philip K. Dick, How to build a Universe, The Marginalian, 1972

[55] Ralph W. Emerson, Brainy Quotes, Facebook.

[56] Ali Bin Abu-Talib, from a poem, Facebook.

8

SLUGGISH DOCTRINE

When I was a young man studying in Austria's capital, Vienna, I was not reflecting upon the Qur'an. I floated, looking for a principle or a religion that I could understand. I found a group of people who had converted to the Mormon doctrine. Some of their information made sense to me, but other things still were not clear. When I questioned the priest with a barrage of inquiries about mysterious things in their faith, he said, "You need to first accept our faith without long thinking. Then you will understand and believe in it."

I was not convinced and did not believe in their faith. If you are confident of the quality of your product, do not hide its specifications. Encourage the buyer to examine, verify, contemplate, and understand what you have to offer.

In the Qur'an, God commands people in many places to use their minds and then believe:

- "Maybe they're wise" is mentioned in the Qur'an twenty-two times
- "They could see" is mentioned thirteen times
- "Those who give thought" is mentioned eleven times
- "Seek to understand the Qur'an" is mentioned twice

However, the divine commands and prohibitions in the holy Qur'an are from the Creator to a creature, who is not equal. God's commands should be applied without controversy. Their advantages may not be known until after application, but we can manage those thoughts in our minds. Dr. Sergei Savilev, a Russian researcher in neurology & others"[57], says that when we think, the brain consume more than 25 percent of the body's energy, because the nerves in the brain are working at full capacity. The brain's energy consumption falls to less than 8 percent if we accept things without careful thinking"[58]. Such a decline can cause decay of the cranial nerves, resulting in the secretion of chemical substances that can numb the brain. This leads to weakness in the mind.

People are of three types:

• Scientists are the ones who are proficient in research.

• Learners or intellectuals are the ones who receive information and experiences from different sources so that they can understand life. Both scientists and learners develop their cognitive abilities, but in different directions.

• The sluggish are those who do not try to understand. They may view what is going on around them, but they accept what is said to them without thinking. The sluggish are many. Sluggish people are easy to drive, like a flock of sheep. They don't use their minds to

---

[57] Marcus E.R. & Debra A.Gusnard, Appraising the Brain's Energy Budget, Pdf, July 29, 2002.

[58] N. Swaminathan, Why does Brain Need so much Power, Pdf, April 29, 2008.

understand what is going on around them or what is said. It is easier for them to accept what other people around them say. Their motto is "If everyone says it and believes it, why do I have to overthink it?"

The sluggish seemingly have concentrated rust in their minds. This rust is the effect of cognitive poverty and reading deprivation. It is mental stagnation. Ceasing to think will make the mind comfortable, and in the colloquial language, we say that this person has a "rusted mind."

Modern philosophy"[59] defines thinking as "**a structured and purposeful cognitive process that we use to understand the world around us to devise decisions.**" Thinking or foresight, which is a fundamental characteristic that God has given to the human mind, develops with the development of our mental awareness. We can use it to solve the problems that face us in this world. We can develop our ability to think in systematic and orderly ways. First, we can focus our attention on everything that goes around us. We can examine our thoughts and other people's ideas on topics of interest to us. Second, we can develop an intellectual sense by practicing our own thinking and learning how others look at a particular topic. This requires a lot of reading and viewing.

Psychology distinguishes types of thinking, including:

- *Traditional or superstitious thinking:* People use superstition or blind imitation to relax their brains. Such thought is simple and naïve. It does not depend on scientific or logical reasoning. This category includes a

---

[59] Steven J. Stein, Emotional Intelligence, E. Book, M. D., 2011.

high percentage of people in society, whom I described above as sluggish.

- *Critical or scientific thinking*: A critical individual relies on the assumptions and opinions of others to challenge assumptions, determine their importance, and reach a conclusion by rational judgment. This category includes many scientists, intellectuals, and learners. This type of thinking increases the energy consumption of the brain, expands it, and creates a mature, creative, and thoughtful human being. This is the thinking that our God always asks of us to strengthen our faith. We should reflect on what we see, which God reminds us of in the holy Qur'an constantly: What is this creature? Why is it the way it is? How does it exist and why? This type of thinking lets us reinforce our faith and be certain of the existence of God, the Creator of everything.

- *Creative or philosophical thinking*: Creative thinking is a process that promotes the development of new and unique ideas for solutions to problems. This category includes inventors who dare to modernize societies, and they are few.

I hope from God that we always remain critical and reflect on all matters in our lives. Reflection can lead us to happier and more fulfilling lives.

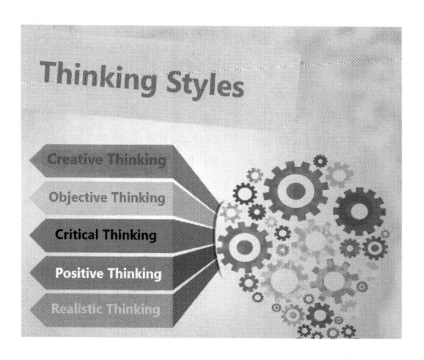

9

THE DESTINY

There are those who ask, "If God has determined my destiny, why would He make me accountable for what I do? And if everything going on in this world happens because God is willing, what is the sin of human beings?"

From my perspective, there is a difference. What a man does is *by his own will*. Fate has nothing to do with it. **The fact that God knows what we are going to do and what will happen does not mean that he imposed it on us.**

Human free will in this worldly life is a trust between God and human beings. All God's other creatures were too afraid to become centers of trust for God. But man wished to have freedom of thought. Therefore, freedom of thought was given only to man. It was formed in our chromosomes in the creation of our grandfather Adam. God made the conscience and intention of man his own. Man is responsible for it, and responsibility is followed by accountability. Other creatures have their natural, God-given instincts and submit to God's will.

God said,

"Every self will be held in pledge for its deeds."[60]

---

[60] Almuddather, verse 38.

God also said,

> "We did indeed offer the Trust to the Heavens and the Earth and the Mountains; but they refused to undertake it, being afraid thereof: but man undertook it, He was indeed unjust and foolish."[61]

The philosopher Freud"[62] said that instinct is raw, and the will of man is controlled by it.

So again the question: Is man free to choose his way, or is he obligated?

One of the pillars of Islam is **to believe in God's destiny, good and evil. God judges and He predestines.** To understand these statements, we must understand the types of influence on human life.

In what follows, I reference the ideas of the Sheikh Mohammed Mutually Al-Sahrawi"[63].

The First Region

Two regions control man's destiny. **God judges and God predestines.** In all that happens to man's **internal organs** or falls on him **from outside**, he has **no choice** and no power. "God simplifies the livelihood for those who want and appreciate."[64]

---

[61] Alahzab, verse 72.
[62] Saul McLeod, Sigmund Freud's Theories, Article 2018
[63] M.M. Al-Sha'rawi, Fate & Predestination, Book, Kindle
[64] Israa',verse 30

God set laws and rules in this world, as I have mentioned. If a human accepts and adheres to these laws, he will be pleased and happy in his life. God will make his life easy, whatever it may be. But if a man breaks the laws, his life will be miserable and hard, even if he acquires money and prestige. God said,

"But whosoever turns away from My Message, verily for him is a life narrowed down, and We shall raise him blind on the Day of Judgment."[65]

But God appreciates a good deed:

"Whoever works righteousness, whether male or female, while being a believer, We will grant him a good life—and We will reward them according to the best of what they used to do."[66]

The Second Region

The second region is proportional with human vision (clairvoyance). The **human being is free**. An act is dictated by the human being **from his will and choice**; his actions are reflections of his own decisions. He is in charge of what happens in his **Self** and is uniquely free in his will. There are no barriers between a man's concealed thoughts and his actions. Your **thoughts** produce your **beliefs**, and your beliefs will produce your **words**. These are followed by your **actions**, which define your **habits**, and your habits describe

---

[65] Taa-Haa, verse 134.
[66] Annahl, verse 97.

your **behavior and character** that lead you to your **destiny**, for good or evil.

When we establish in ourselves the control of our desires—which God has placed in our religion and our good nature—we initiate the happiness that we were promised by God. We become masters of ourselves, not slaves to our desires. The Creator's words are clear in the following verse:

> "So, he who gives in charity and fears Allah, and testifies to the best, We will indeed make smooth for him the path to Bliss. But he who is a greedy miser and thinks himself sufficient, and gives the lie to the best, We will indeed make smooth for him the path to Misery."[67]

This means that **God always leaves us the freedom of initiative and action with our intention**. Then God's will come with his justice. He will bestow guidance or misdirection on us according to our intention. This means that God's destiny is the product of the self's intention.

God granted us part of the freedom we wanted. Thus, he imposed on us a great responsibility for our actions. It is a freedom to be responsible for what we do. Responsibility is followed by evaluation and accounting.

In conclusion, human freedom is real, despite the limits and resistances that can exist around it.

We traditionally think of money and status as success. It is a method of evaluation and an examination by God in this

---

[67] Allyl, verse 10.

life. The same is true of poverty and need; these are also an assessment and an examination. God says,

> "Now, as for the man, when his Lord trieth him, giving him honor and gifts, then saith he: 'My Lord hath honored me', But when He trieth him restricting his subsistence for him, then saith he: 'My Lord hath humiliated me', Nay."[68]

Injustice, jealousy, envy, gambling, and malice abuse are degrees of suicide, wasting life and freedom. Then God leads us to unhappiness. For example:

- A worker neglects the work assigned to him. Result? He's out of his job.
- A trader cheats with his wares. Result? His wares stop selling.
- A man speaks words that are lies. Result? He will be known to God and to his associates as a liar. He will lose people's trust and respect.
- A manager is unjust to his workers. Result? His workers will be insincere in their work.

If I want to burn a house, I'm the one who puts a matchstick to the house. The fire begins to work. That is a chemical law created by God between material and oxygen. But I am the one who decided to burn the house; it was not God's will.

If you thank God for who you are, be merciful to God's creatures. Seek good for all. Leave backbiting, gossip, cunning,

---

[68] Alfajr, verses 15–17.

and what angers God. Seek God's pleasure. That will bring you goodness, comfort, reassurance, and happiness in all the circumstances of your life, because God will love you and take care of you.

10

THE DIVINE BOOK

The holy Qur'an is the word of God Almighty. It is not a creature—as claimed by the Mu'tazila in the ninth century, during the days of the Caliph Al-Mammon—because God's creatures have a lifetime and end. I look at the Qur'an as a miracle painting; every word and letter in its position has a special meaning. The Qur'an contains thousands of images that God created. It portrays science, morals, exhortations, and advice to the world from the past to the future. No one can completely interpret them except God, but in each human era, we can work on interpreting the Qur'an by reflecting on the meanings of each verse and how those meanings apply to that era. God said,

> "But no one knows its hidden meaning except Allah, and those who are firmly grounded in knowledge say: We believe in the book all is from our Lord, and only people of understanding remember."[69]

Therefore, the noble Qur'an is an eternal book for every time and place. I believe that it is difficult to understand the thought in the Qur'an for all eras **except for the firm**

[69] Al-Emran, verse 7.

and constant laws, such as acts of worship, inheritance, the attitude of religion toward women and orphans, and the consultation process in general matters of the people, such as choosing a ruler.

Nevertheless, we are able to understand the reflections of the verses' meanings. Many honorable interpreters—with God's help—have worked hard and given us some ambiguous or unclear meanings of some verses, which they interpreted according to their era but are difficult to be convinced of today. The Almighty said:

> "For every massage is a limit of time, and soon shall ye know it".[70]

> "And ye shall certainly know the truth of it after a while."[71]

> "Praise be to Allah, Who will soon show you His Signs."[72]

Nobody can interpret the Qur'an in the literal sense, even if that person possesses huge amounts of information about the Arabic language, hadith, natural science, psychology, sociology, life sciences, and so on. But we can perceive some thoughts and opinions.

The Qur'an is a book of religion, and it is a *way of life* for a decent way of living. It is not a book of philosophy. It suffices

---

[70] Alana'am, verse 67.

[71] Alnaml, verse 93.

[72] S~ad, verse 88.

with *flashing, ablution, hint, symbol,* and *signs* in most of its verses and stories.

I have heard those who claim that some Qur'an verses are contradictory. This is because the claimant did not understand the semantic limits of the words of the Qur'an and did not understand the words' connotations. Studying the meanings of Qur'anic vocabulary is an important step toward better understanding the anthropology of Qur'an. Every word used in the Qur'an has semantic limits that we can explore and draw. For example, the word "man" does not have quite the same meaning as "people" or "human being." The word "person" is not quite the same as "son of Adam" or "self." Every word has semantic limits.

When I meditate on the Qur'an and look at the interpretations of some interpreters, pleasant thoughts come to my mind. Is the method and terminology of the hereafter understandable as it is in this world? Of course not, because in the hereafter there is Horon Een (mere eye ladies), and rivers of milk and honey. What if someone cannot tolerate honey? Is there an account of time in the Hereafter? Will we grow old? Will we get hungry?

Each dynamic system has a different time than any other dynamic system. That's why time in one's life differs from that in the hereafter. When we enter a dream as we sleep, the time we experience is not the same as during a period of waking vigilance. In a dream, we may be exposed to events and information that take time over years, but the time that passes in the waking world is probably less than half an hour.

Since God created humans, He sent down other divine books and the Qur'an as guidance for a decent way of living in this world of testing. But after judgment day, this approach may not apply!

Before Prophet Mohammad, peace upon him, God sent messengers to every nation with instructions and a simplified approach that suited their cognitive ability and their living conditions. Prophet Mohammad's message was the overall message and the conclusion of the line of messengers.

Understanding of the thoughts in a Quranic verse is according to the scientific and cultural level of those who seek to understand their significance. Human understanding guides the seeker to the thoughts and methods that can lead them to a happier life. People of past times were guided to thoughts and understandings about certain verses according to their cultural and scientific level. As for the people of the present, we have deconstructed other meanings and thoughts. Our grandchildren and great-grandchildren will discover other thoughts and connotations that will help guide them into a better life.

Some may say that the holy Qur'an is all talk about fire, torment, and woe. Yes, there are a lot of warnings to those who do not understand or think. It contains more verses of great meaning and wisdom. It contains scientific miracles for those who understand and reason. The Creator describes those who doubt His miracles, saying, "But none reject our signs except only a perfidious wretch."[73]

The number of verses in the noble Qur'an is 6,236. There are 535 verses of legislation and about 1,395 verses discussing science, knowledge, vision, and remembrance of the miracles that God has created in and around us. As for what is left, those

---

[73] Luqman, verse 32.

verses mostly touch on real stories of people who have passed through this life. There are also sermons and contemplations of God's judgment.

God has set instinct in the formation of man's chromosomes since the time of our grandfather Adam. From him, this code was passed on to all the nations in the world. Every characteristic of this instinct has a cause and purpose. To eat an apple, we must plant an apple tree, and eating apples is necessary for our growth. Likewise, to multiply, we must find a partner, and sex is an instinct.

God also set in his Qur'an regulations and laws the fine-tuning of every aspect of instinct. For example, our Lord advises us not to respond badly to those who offend us. He says,

"Repel with what is better: then will he between whom and thee was hatred become as it were thy friend and intimate."[74]

The world of the hereafter is a different world. Reasons do not need a cause. You will live forever and not age. You do not need to grow or multiply. If you want an apple, you can make that feeling in your mouth. Many things are difficult for our human brains to comprehend now. Only God knows.

The laws of the hereafter are not the same as the laws of the existing world. In the holy Qur'an, our Lord has set for us a *simulation* of what we will be in heaven and hell, so we can try to understand the situation in the hereafter. The fire of the hereafter may not be like the fire of this world. The fire of this world is a simulation to make it easier for us to understand

---

[74] Fuselat, verse 34.

the meaning. On earth, humans need the power of faith in God, His books, and the last day without having the ability to understand all the details.

And God knows better. God said,

> "With him are the keys of unseen, the treasures that none knows but He."[75]

But if we believe that the noble Qur'an is from God, we must believe in the occult that God has told us about:

> "Who believe in the unseen, are steadfast in prayer... they are on true guidance, and it is these who will prosper."[76]

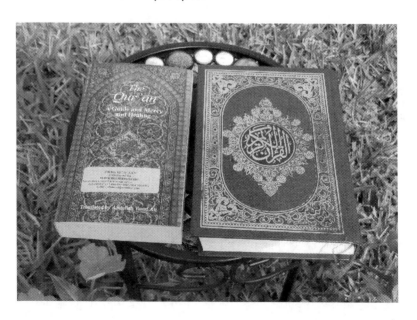

---

[75] Alan'am, verse 59.
[76] Al Bakara, verses 3–5.

11

LAWS OF LIFE

Why does one person become rich and another poor?

Why does one person succeed in reaching what he wants and another fails?

Why is that man happy and I am unfortunate?

We live in a universe that the Creator created with laws and balance in everything. Those laws are signs for people who contemplate. To answer the previous questions, we must understand the laws of life, of science, of morality, of energy in the human self, and so on.

For example, the laws of arithmetic state that two times three equals six. The result cannot be seven or five! According to the laws of physics, light travels in a straight line. According to the laws of chemical reactions, $2H_2{}^+{}_g + O^-{}_g = H_2O$. According to the laws of the universe, the sun and the moon each follow their own orbits. According to the laws of morality, if you smile in my face, I will smile in your face. If you lie to me, then I will lose confidence in you. If you intend harm toward me, harm will reflect on you sooner or later.

All these laws are absolutes. They are unbiased with regard to race, color, or religion. The laws do not differentiate between a believer and a nonbeliever.

Dr. Eng. Fahim JAUHARY

The Almighty said:

"It is Allah Who has sent down the Book in Truth and the Balance."[77]

"And the Firmament has He raised high, and He has set up the Balance."[78]

God created everything in balance, He said,

"We sent afore time our messengers with clear signs and sent down with them the Book and the Balance."[79]

God created all things in due balance:

"And the earth We have spread out, set thereon mountains firm and immovable, and produced therein all kinds of things in due Balance."[80]

The Creator also tells us that He created all pairs in balance between male and female:

"Glory to Allah, Who created in pairs all things that the earth produces, as well as their kind and things of which they do not know."[81]

---

[77] Ashora, verse 17.
[78] Alrahman, verse 7.
[79] Alhadeed, verse 25.
[80] Alhijr, verse 19.
[81] Yaseen, verse 36.

Likewise, God created stars and moons to move in specific motions, in a rhythm resembling the oscillating motion of a boat:

"And He (God) who created the Night, the Day, the Sun and the Moon, each in an Orbit are swimming."[82]

The self also has an absolute law of gravity between one person and another—the law of attraction, as it is called. This law does not only apply to the physical attraction between astronomical bodies but also applies to the attraction between different human bodies.

Since objects have energy, attraction stems from the energy present in a body. The strength of attraction is directly proportional to the product of the mass of two objects divided by the square of the distance between them. The moon revolves around the earth, and the earth revolves around the sun. Centrifugal force will keep the moon away from the earth and the earth away from the sun. The more the center of attraction loses part of its energy, the farther away the attracted object will be. For example, after thousands of years, one earth day might increase to twenty-five hours instead of twenty-four. One solar year might become thirteen months instead of twelve. These are the laws of God the Creator.

Likewise, there are laws of energy: sound, light, and rays. Energy consists of frequency waves or vibrations that have a distinct length, width, and speed, such as the energy emitted by the mobile phones that we carry.

---

[82] Alanbia', verse 33.

I believe that the self is a type of energy that can change its frequency, attraction, or broadcast. Each self has special waves. But God knows best.

The human point of reception and transmission to the frequencies of ideas is the subconscious mind, as defined by psychologists"[83]. As we think, we consume energy and transmit it in certain forms. An image will be printed in our subconscious and transmit on certain frequencies. The image can be a well-liked image or an evil image. Whenever we change the image in ourselves, the frequencies we transmit will change.

The Prophet (pbuh) said, "Be optimistic, you find the good."[84]

Have you ever noticed that what you need may happen to you? Or maybe someone you were thinking of suddenly appears in front of you? Have you ever been in the right place at the wrong time? You might have found your life partner and been surprised that they were in one way or another connected to your life or acquaintance circle without your prior knowledge?

All these are proofs that the law of attraction works in our lives. We can define the law of attraction as **the law that attracts ideas into your life that dominate your mind either positively or negatively"[85].**

---

[83] Joseph Murphy, The power of your subconscious Mind, Book, 1981, Amazon, CA, USA

[84] Binbaz.org.sa/fatwas.

[85] Brian Tracy, Proven Process for Success, Audio Book, Amazon.

The pictures in our imaginations"[86] could be the money we always wanted, the way we collect that money, the certification we aspire to achieve, the misery we are in, and so one. From what I have just mentioned, I affirm that there is **nothing in life that we call luck or coincidence.** Belief in chance is nothing but an excuse used by losers. Everything that takes place around us follows laws established by the Creator of this life. Everything that happens in existence or in us is subject to the frequencies emitted by our minds, good or bad. So, to be happy, we must hold our thoughts accountable to ourselves and others. Is it good or bad?

Human personality is within the person. It is the values and the principles a person sets for himself. It is the concepts that are difficult to change. Personality determines our behavior and actions, which we can change depending on different situations.

Many philosophers discuss the relationship between human thoughts and actions, and between a person's personality and behavior. **Our thoughts define our personalities, which become words. Words turn into actions that in turn constitute habits and behavior, which in turn determine one's destiny** by interacting with the universe in various pleasant and difficult circumstances. From this, I conclude that there is **neither luck nor coincidence.**

---

[86] John Assaraf, How I bought my dream House, You Tube Video, Apr. 6,2016

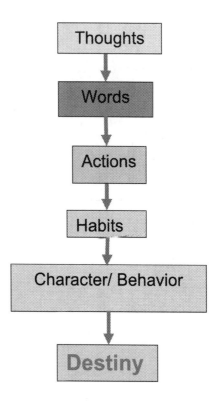

Science has not yet been able to obtain many details about the secrets and types of transmitters and receivers for the physical and psychological forces of attraction and expulsion. Nevertheless, we must understand how to intelligently use them to our advantage.

For example, the law of gravity is the reason why water flows from higher points to lower points. Human beings can use the potential energy stored in the higher water to produce electric energy as it flows down, making their lives better. On the other hand, a man who does not respect his life and is inconsiderate to God might throw himself from a great height, such as the top of a building, and empty the potential energy stored in his body by dying.

What kinds of thoughts are in your subconscious and conscious mind? If we continue to think positively and dream—perhaps by assuring ourselves that we will become rich without over worrying and while working hard to achieve our goal—we will, after a while, become rich. But when wealth becomes a property in our hands, we might become haunted by fears of losing it. This can lead us back to poverty or, perhaps, to living a miserable life overthinking it.

That is why our thoughts must always be positive. We should believe and praise God Almighty and not fear poverty. Always expect what you want. Do not expect what you do not want. Always thank God for what He has given you. God said,

"Your Lord caused to be declared: If ye are grateful, I will add more unto you, but if ye show ingratitude, truly My punishment is terrible indeed."[87]

As for when calamity happens to a person without his willing it, that is a test from God. God knows best his wisdom.

When I was fifty years old, I received the diagnosis of rheumatoid arthritis and started walking with crutches. Climbing stairs was hard, and I couldn't even carry a thin, smooth paper between my fingers. I checked into the hospital and became a prisoner of many treatments. I was told that this disease would reach my lungs and heart, and that would be the end. I said

---

[87] Ibrahim, verse 7.

to my wife, "My dream was to travel the world with you when I retire, but it seems that will not happen."

Months passed. I convinced myself that I would be stronger than the disease. I insisted, despite the pain, on standing without help, eating my food, and drinking. I tried to play sports and live happily. I was sure that I would overcome the disease because I trusted my God first and then trusted myself second. I was not afraid of any result.

Many years later, I am now over eighty years old, the disease has almost disappeared, and I'm now traveling the world!

Any incurable disease can be treated from within oneself by following the right regimen of diet, physical activity, and medication. Man is the product of his thoughts.

Law of cause & reason
Nothing happened by chance,
every action pays off,
even after a while

12

POWER OF THE
SUBCONSCIOUS MIND

The human brain works in two lines:

- *The conscious mind* controls logical thinking. It chooses and decides willingly. Using the conscious mind, a man determines what suits him, decides what he wants, and ponders what he believes in. He is the director, guiding and processing the world through five senses. The conscious mind only works when the human being is awake.

- *The inner or subconscious mind* accepts everything that is given to it. It believes without thinking or analysis. It is like the soil of the earth, which the conscious mind cultivates. The subconscious works twenty-four hours a day. It supervises the work of the body's vital organs, such as the heart, lungs, and stomach.

I read the book *The Power of Your Subconscious Mind* by the scientist Joseph Murphy"[88]. It talks about the power of the subconscious mind (unconscious mind) and delves into the

---

[88] Joseph Murphy, The power of your subconscious Mind, Book, 1981, Amazon, CA, USA.

details of the influence of the subconscious mind on human life. According to Murphy, a man can utilize it to achieve what he wishes.

Murphy presents a tremendous number of practical experiences and discusses various ways that human consciousness can convince the subconscious to achieve a specific desire. But I was not fully convinced of the psychological justifications he gives. My wife reminded me of a verse from the Qur'an:

> "For each such person, there are angels in succession, before and behind him: they guard him by command of Allah. Allah does not change a person's lot unless they change what in their selves."[89]

What comes to my mind here is that God ordered angels to guard human beings (believer and unbeliever). These angels are commanded by the human subconscious mind (good or evil). **The subconscious mind then has supernatural abilities beyond human limits through the help of these angels.**

If you have good intentions, you will succeed. If you have ill intentions, you will lose. God will not change what is in you unless you change what is within yourself. Faith and desire stem from the conscious mind. The subconscious mind believes what the conscious mind believes and executes its desires with the help of the angels. These are things beyond human imagination, but they happen.

---

[89] Al-Raad, verse 11.

God knows better.

I don't know how it's done, but I am convinced of it. I have personally experienced such cases. Some were performed consciously and with persistence on my end, and some were the result of internal desire without insistence. If we examine what is going on around us, we realize that there is an effect described by that noble Quranic verse, and its meaning becomes clear. The problem is how to convince your subconscious mind of something. How is the technique of persuasion performed?

Here is an experience that happened to me. When I was in the final stages of my PhD research, my mind was completely occupied day and night looking for solution to a specific problem. I woke up one day and was still half asleep. Suddenly a funny, illogical solution to the problem popped up in my mind. When I went to the lab, I wanted to cheer up my mentor professor, and I told him my dream solution. I was surprised when he assured me that it was a logical solution. I applied it and finished my research.

Our conscious minds think, decide, and feel by our five senses. While our subconscious minds do not recognize place or time, the subconscious realizes what is around it with the clairvoyance sense (the ability to gain information about an object through extrasensory perception). When the five senses are not ready, the subconscious mind uses clairvoyance. It can leave your body and travel. It can dive into the feelings of others and imagine them. The information is stored in the subconscious as in a computer—if it wants to remember, then it chooses from its library of video for a relevant case. It can study that video to find a suitable solution to a problem.

The subconscious mind is convinced of what the conscious mind dictates and confirms. For example, if I want to become something, I have to convince my subconscious mind that I can do so and reassure it repeatedly. This relationship is only between my conscious and subconscious mind; it is not between me and someone else, and it is not wise to broadcast it to others. I should focus on what I want. **People who make their own reality are not afraid of the future, because they know that their reality will be similar to what they have drawn with their subconscious.**

Believe you are able to achieve anything you work for. Believe from the depths within you that you will become rich and successful, or will recover from a disease. That is the magic key for getting what you want. If you believe that you are unhappy, you will become truly unhappy. This is a real operation, but we don't know how it works. Yes, there is magic in the faith of your subconscious mind. Of course, this work is not easy; it requires training and mental focus.

Hard work alone does not lead you to success, but hard work with faith will lead you to reach your goal. Clearly place what you want in your conscious mind. Prepare your potential and draw its chart. Be serious and patient. Your thoughts will pass on to your subconscious mind, and this will attract what you are interested in.

The infinite intelligence of the subconscious mind directs us spiritually, mentally, and materially. Murphy lists many examples. One is a fifty-year-old woman who had never previously thought about getting married. All of a sudden, she was completely occupied with the thought of marriage. The urgency of that dream continued and occupied her for weeks. Then her dream came true.

Here I must mention my personal experience when I was a pilgrim in Mecca. Zamzam Well is located inside the courtyard of Kaaba, which is in a desert area, seventy-two kilometers from the sea. The well has an ancient history dating back to the time of Prophet Abraham. The well has continuously pumped potable water since then, and currently has a capacity of up to eighteen liters per second. Zamzam water is considered carbonated water. It is very rich in minerals, with two thousand milligrams per liter. Its pH is 7.8. Zamzam water is blessed for Muslims. Prophet Mohammad said, "Zamzam water is the best water on the face of the earth, in food that tastes good, and as a cure for illness"[90]. On my hajj, I had to circumambulate the Kaaba, a walk of more than ten kilometers. Before the end of the circumambulation, I became so tired that I was unable to continue. I fell to the ground. My wife was told that if she washed my feet with Zamzam water, I would come back and complete the trip. I believed it, and it was done. I ultimately became active and resumed my walking.

In another case, Prophet Mohammad, the Messenger of God, told his companions that they would conquer the Persian and the Roman empires. Although they were nomads, they believed in the dream and worked on it, and it was ultimately achieved.

If the conscious mind believes in something, the subconscious mind will act accordingly. **How do I ask my unconscious mind to do something?**

I sit in a quiet, secluded place, close my eyes, and relax for some time. I focus on each of my body members (legs, hands,

---

[90] Mohammad Shodab, Zamzam Water, Prophet Honest talks, Mar 28, 2019

heart) one by one and ask them to relax until I reach a dozing state. I tell myself to be sure of the beautiful fact that everything I ask can be implemented. God created me and made me better. I repeat this affirmation in a faint, low voice until I truly believe that my request will be fulfilled,

I repeat this process for days or even weeks. If I trust and believe in the reality of any idea and work on it, it will become a reality.

13

SECRET OF RELIANCE ON GOD

Throughout the ages, humans have encountered difficulties and problems. The most difficult problems are the ones we are facing in this era. This is the age of evolution, technology, nanotechnology, and quantum mechanics. Many believe that modern science helps solve human psychological problems, but the opposite is true. Science in schools, universities, and modern philosophy has not been able to prevent the spread of lies, fraud, drugs, crime, insecurity, anxiety, and fear.

Recently, I read a heartbreaking story in the newspaper. A groom got angry and suffocated his bride on the night of their wedding.

Differences of opinion between one person and another are normal, but to act on such differences with violence or screaming is inhumane. When animals get angry, they use their hands, legs, and teeth because their clairvoyance is nonexistent. They are underthinking by instinct. God did not blow them out of His soul. He gave them the self and instinct to grow and multiply and preserve their sex.

Life's problems are endless, and we are required to solve them daily. What are the reasons? Are physical solutions enough?

> ➤ Are alcohol and other drugs the solution? Their use makes the problem worse. The only winners are the dealer and the psychiatrist.

> ➤ Is money a solution? Rich people and rich countries are not helped by money; rather, money becomes a burden on them. Among the rich, there is a lot of luxury, drugs, and false pride, leading to corruption. Money security is a hoax.

> ➤ Maybe technology and science are solutions? Universities do not prevent the spread of fear, anxiety, insecurity, and crime. The unscrupulous misuse of technology leads to problems.

> ➤ Maybe intelligence is a solution? Unfortunately, sometimes man uses his intelligence to exploit others, increase vileness in wars, and conquer his brother.

All of these are *material solutions* or physical methods. They do not rely on God and or on acting according to His right guidance on how to live. Therefore, they do not represent the best solutions to the problems of this world. Drugs, money, science, intelligence, and philosophy all use the tangible material of the nature of our physical formation and *ignore or fail to recognize our spiritual composition*. They falsely claim that nature formed itself.

> ❖ What if we look at faith in the Creator, who guarantees everything He created? Faith in our God is open to all human beings—no commitments, no expenses.

> ❖ God created the believer, the disobedient, and the nonbeliever, ensuring their livelihoods. *God loves all His creations*, Muslim and non-Muslim. He is merciful

to them on different levels. He is merciful with the obedient, the hard-working, and even the nonbeliever, although he does not cherish the unbeliever and does not satisfy him in his disbelief.

❖ Yes, let's deal with beliefs which enter our selves— refining them, satisfying them, and giving them safety. Those beliefs *become a tangible fact.*

God said,

"It is those who believe and confuse not their beliefs with wrong – that are truly in security, for they are on right guidance."[91]

God said,

"Who provides them with food against hunger and with security against fear."[92]

Many recognize that God truly exists. But it is difficult for them to understand how relying on God is essential. This is because they have a jumble of worldly, material affairs in their minds. They are confused!

God sent apostles and messengers to the people. Those messengers brought evidence to help the people believe in God and be guided. In order to believe in something, your mind must first be sure of it. *Certainty proves the faith.* Confirming the existence of the Creator of this universe are the miracles described in the Qur'an, which is revealed from God. The

---

[91] Alan'am, verse 82.

[92] Quraish, verse 4.

Qur'an has existed for more than 1,400 years. It was brought into the world in a desert region, where people had neither scientific experience nor knowledge of the universe. *The Qur'an's approach depends on faith to prove certainty.* Islam is not like other beliefs. The Muslim's faith depends on understanding with his mind and his awareness. Islam asks us to use our brains. If we recognize the logic, certainty is proven. Certainty is the confidence in or conviction of the existence of a greater power that created this universe—a power that sent prophets and the Qur'an to guide people to islam. Certainty means trusting in the existence of God. It is an inner feeling in humans.

We must learn certainty and its practice to improve our belief in God and to fully depend on Him. God is knowledgeable about everything and manages everything. He manages justice and destiny. He left us to use our minds within the borders He drew for us, and He asked us to trust Him.

God said,

> "This is the creation of God, so show me what those besides Him have created, rather the wrongdoers are in clear error."[93]

Prophet Mohammad said: "Learn certainty as you learn the Qur'an until you knew it, I am learning it."[94]

Relying on God is a beautiful feeling. The feeling gives one reassurance and acceptance of what will be, even if it is not what one wants it to be. I do not claim that religion is the opium of the masses, because opium stops the mind from

---

[93] Luqman, verse 11.

[94] Sahih Al-Bukhari, ISBN-13:978-1567445190, Maktba Dar-US-Islam

working. The Qur'an demands the use of the mind, and it considers opium and alcohol evil. I say that faith is a beautiful feeling with logic; it changes the self and delights it. It is only realized by those who deepen their faith in certainty and learn the following:

- If you believe that God will make you happy, and you follow His approach, you'll be happy.
- If you believe that God will give you success in your work, and you follow His approach, you're going to be successful.
- If you believe that God will save you from a miserable or sick situation, and you follow his approach, you surely will be saved.
- Believe that everything you don't have was never originally meant for you.
- Believe that all that God has given you is a mercy to you, and what is withheld from you is wisdom.

There's no such thing as coincidence, nor does one succeed through one's own effort or intelligence. Yes, there is no doubt that personal effort and intelligence are factors in one's success—and perhaps in one's failures! But God frames one's destiny and appreciates the results.

The product of your effort and intelligence will satisfy you if you abide by faith in God, because God will appreciate what satisfies you. Yes, there are rich infidels, and we think that they are successful. But God is testing them. If you looked inside them, you would see they are unsatisfied for one reason or another.

Belief in God is the key to success for a reassured self. Believe that God is your sponsor. Return to Him in your affairs. Accept what you are destined to have and be thankful. Belief in God and his Messengers and reliance on God are equivalent to ending psychological problems and softening the impact of physical or material problems.

The life of this world is like a playhouse. It is also a house of happiness and a test for you from your Creator. So God created the filthy rich and the thankful contented. A poor nonbeliever might be dissatisfied while another is satisfied. There are miserable believers and happy believers. God has left you the choice of what you want to be, to test you.

There are many examples of people who have inherited and then lost a lot of money, or who have lived unhappily despite having riches. People born poor were enriched by God or happy despite their poverty. Some people have everything they wish for, but they are miserable. They may even commit suicide.

God said,

> "Verily those who say: Our Lord is Allah and remains firm; on them shall be no fear, nor shall they grieve."[95]

Also God reassures believers. He said,

> "It is those who believe and confuse not their beliefs with wrong – that are truly in security, for they are on right guidance."[96]

---

[95] Alahqaf, verse 13.

[96] Alana'am, verse 82.

Reality is that which,
when you stop believing
in it, doesn't go away"

Philip K. Dick

14

PHILOSOPHY AND RELIGION

Philosophy is a tool of science, knowledge, and thought activity. Islam is the religion of life. It does not need philosophy because it is clear.

Humans have practiced philosophy and jurisprudence from ancient times, searching for truth, the facts of life, and the world's Creator. Philosophy is said to be the daughter of religions and the mother of science. In philosophy, man usually seeks the roots of real knowledge. He wants to be convinced and to learn how to persuade. Realistic knowledge is a true belief, justified by work. Facts are valued by work. Facts are to our brains as food is to our bodies. Some facts are more delicious than others to our cognitive sensitivity. Knowledge gives you pleasure, so man is always seeking the truth.

The Greek philosopher Aristotle believed that there must be a first reason that created everything, and thus created existence and time. Plato described the Creator as an example of ultimate goodness. There are two worlds: our imperfect real world, which we live in, and another perfect world with replicas of our world. Philosophers have continued to search for existence even until this day. The reason is that man, under the pressure of his longing to know the Creator, always seeks Him through philosophy, even though God has sent every nation messengers dedicated to God.

Some believe that without philosophy, we would not know the Creator"[97]. But I am sure that by contemplating the great Qur'an, we will be convinced of the existence of the Creator. The Qur'an does not need a philosophy; it is all knowledge, intellectual activity, clear facts, and action. Its verses describe scientific facts and realistic images, showing us the roots of knowledge. Those who think about and understand the Qur'an are convinced, whether they are scientists, scholars, or ordinary people.

Islam is distinct from philosophy. It is the religion of real life. The message of Islam, which descended on Prophet Mohammad, is a realistic doctrine. It is deeper knowledge than philosophy, encompassing all the realities of life in the world and the hereafter. Its laws respect all that God has created and transcend the limits of the human mind. It surpassed its predecessors in religion and philosophy, as found among the people of Greece, India, and China. This is the secret behind the speed of its spread at the beginning of the message. However, this spread has encountered and continues to face difficulties. These difficulties are mainly **due to people who claim to understand religion and yet consider a Muslim who researches the application of the** jurisprudence of reality **in Quranic verses to be a nonbeliever.**

For example, some of the old scholars focused on making sure to dress just like the Prophet did. But God praised the morals of the Prophet, not his clothes, meaning that the focus of a believer should be on morals, not dress. Some have even gone as far as prohibiting banking transactions, or the study of anatomy in medicine. They create difficulty and complications

---

[97] Iben Roshd, History of Islam Philosophers, Hindawi.org/Books.

by viewing further research into religion as taboo. There are those who interpreted some verses of Qur'an wrongly"[98], Because of them, some people refrain from believing in religion.

I do not deny that many of our Muslim ancestors in many villages and cities have understood the holy Qur'an and lived with it as ordered by the Lord of the worlds. Many have dedicated their lives to serving Islam.

I believe that after the era of the rightly guided top four caliphs, those who conveyed the meanings of religion to us in good faith resorted to the traditional style of preaching. They delved into the interpretation of metaphysical issues in unconvincing ways. They were strict about the provisions of the religion to the point of atonement, believing in superstitions and forbidding music of all kinds. They created ideologies about life as a source of misery, or that women are lacking in intelligence. They said that women should be covered in black and their place is only at home, while a man can marry four women without conditions, and many more. They even went as far as cancelling the "Shura law" (self-government by we the people), which is based on consulting the general Muslim population before choosing a ruler. They stayed away from applying the correct teachings of the Qur'an and from explaining its material facts.

Consequently, many young people came to believe that they are toys in the hands of destiny—that they are powerless. Our God in the Qur'an tells us that every self is held accountable for what it does. The human being is honored and is God's successor on earth. God asks us to work so that God and His

---

[98] Al-Jalalayn, Tafsir, Book by Al-Mahalli & Al-Suyuti, i.e Al-gashiah, verse 20.

Messenger see our work. Every human is responsible for his work and is rewarded for it in this world and the hereafter. God commands justice, equality, and human rights in this world. As for the accountability of the wrongdoer, it will happen on the Day of Judgment before God. **Unfortunately, the goals of the Islamic religion have been misunderstood. Some Muslims became dependent, abandoning life development, work, and research into the roots of knowledge.** They surrendered their affairs to fate. Often when the truth is blind, it is a danger to human beliefs.

Some old books with that type of content are dry, devoid of the spirit of worldly life and looking only at spirituality. Their facts are blind. They exaggerate violations and prohibitions, adding what they were accustomed to from their closed society or what were dictated to them in customs and traditions. Their writers did not realize the true meanings of the Qur'an, in that God revealed it as guidance for His people. The Qur'an is meant **to make people happy in this world as in the hereafter,** and to organize good and loving relations among all humans, animals, plants, and inanimate creatures.

God said,

"There is no compulsion in religion, for truth has emerged from error."[99]

In our present world, we think about and deal with systems, scales, and dimensions specific to our existing world. A day represents the rotation of the earth around itself, but will the earth rotate in paradise? A meter has an agreed length in the

---

[99] Al-Baqara, verse 256.

world, and size is measured in three dimensions: length, width, and height. To locate a point, we deal with four dimensions, which are length, width, height, and time. We must manage and adhere to what we are asked in our real world. As for the supernatural forces mentioned in the holy Qur'an and in some of the hadiths of the Messenger, they may have other systems and dimensions that we cannot visualize, making them difficult for us to perceive. They are examples of simulation and consideration, but we accept their thoughts as they are.

For example, God said:

"Allah is the light of heaven and the earth."[100]

"Be quick in the race.... and for gardens whose width is that of heavens and the earth prepared for the righteous."[101]

"Those who reject our signs ...As often as their skins are roasted through; We shall change them for fresh skins".[102]

Other examples are hard to imagine:

"Their light will run forward before them and their right hands".[103]

---

[100] Alnoor, verse 35.
[101] Al Imran, verse 133.
[102] Anisa, verse 56.
[103] Altahreem, verse 8.

"I do call to what you see, and what you see not."[104]

"On a Day, space whereof will be as a thousand years of your reckoning."[105]

"Then we send her our angel and he appeared before her as a man in all respects."[106]

"So, and we shall join them to fair women with beautiful, big, and lustrous eyes."[107]

We must accept such examples as we receive them, without frills and without comparing them to what exists in our world.

Qur'an tells us scientific facts and realistic images, showing us the roots of knowledge. Those who think and understand it are convinced whether they are: scientists, scholars, or living on the street.

---

[104] Alhaqa, verses 38–39.
[105] Sajda, verse 5.
[106] Maryam, verse 17.
[107] Dhukhan, verse 54.

15

DOCTRINE OF REALITY

After the era of the rightly guided top four caliphs, Muslims were under the rule of other Islamic caliphs, such as the Umayyad, Abbasid, and Ottoman. These caliphs failed often and deviated from the thoughts of the Qur'an. They failed to develop correct meanings in proportion to the development of human understanding.

The holy Qur'an is in clear Arabic language. It calls for good morals and for staying away from bad behaviors. It calls for respect for others, care for animal welfare, and chastity. **The believer loves God and God loves the believer. The believer is humbled in front of God. He is not afraid of death, because he will be in the hands of his Creator. He leaves fear of fire to the nonbeliever.**

God has created mankind with different ethnicities and races in various colors and traditions. Humans are distinct from one another in fingerprints and eye prints, no matter their degree of belief.

God said:

> "If thy Lord had so willed, He could have made mankind One People: but they Will not cease to dispute."[108]

---

[108] Hood, verse 118.

"It is He who created you, and among you is the disbeliever, and among you is the believer. And Allah, of what you do, is Seeing."[109]

We are to treat each other with respect, as a great human family that feels the unity of human origin. God said,

"And let there be [arising] from you a nation inviting to [all that is] good, enjoining what is right and forbidding what is wrong, and those will be the successful."[110]

The following verse gives any person the freedom to be a Muslim without coercion, because the truth is clear. God said,

"There shall be no compulsion in [acceptance of] the religion. The right course has become distinct from the wrong. So whoever disbelieves in ṭāghūt [juggernaut] and believes in Allah has grasped the most trustworthy handhold with no break in it. And Allah is Hearing and Knowing."[111]

That is, one person is not allowed to force another person to embrace a particular idea or doctrine. You can practice any religion or not practice a religion.

---

[109] Al-Taghabun, verse 2.
[110] Al-Omran, verse 104.
[111] Albaqara, verse 256.

Fighting is allowed only for those who have experienced oppression and were robbed unjustly of their money, family, or beliefs.

God said,

> "So whoever has assaulted you, then assault him in the same way that he has assaulted you. And fear Allah and know that Allah is with those who fear Him."[112]

Since the distinguished scholars of Islam began to interpret the holy Qur'an in order to clarify the words of God, these interpretations have differed somewhat. Differences are due to the varying opinions of those scholars and according to their era, place, specialties, and interests, ignoring basic principles upon which Islam is based. Although the Arabic language of the Qur'an is clear, Arabic is a broad language, but it is accurate expressions in the choice of words.

In addition, some special verses in Qur'an were revealed for a specific occasion and should not be applied to every situation.

For example, God said in a specific occasion:

> "And kill them wherever you overtake them and expel them from wherever they have expelled you."[113]

In every era and sect, interpreters discovered understandable interpretations for their people. **All interpretations of the**

---

[112] Albaqara, verse 194.
[113] Al-Baqara, verse 191.

Qur'an are good for their era, but they do not replace the actual Qur'an. The Qur'an is the only source of Islamic legislation for every age and time. It should be the religious base for any group of Muslim scholars and people in any era. To understand what is meant by a Quranic verse, we should differentiate between good and bad behavior for our era and place, in a way that does not contradict God's regulations. God said, in the words of Luqman advising his son,

"O my son! Establishes the prayer, order with the well-known good but forbid dishonor, and bear patiently with whatever may fall upon you, that is of steadfast heart of things."[114]

Unfortunately, many of the books published in the modern era continue to convey the interpretations of an ancient era, interpretations that were valid only for that era. Ancient interpretations lack careful consideration and understanding of the doctrine of reality. The holy Qur'an is valid for every time and place if we understand its basic principles and thoughts.

As an example: our Sheikh Al-sha'rawi, may God have mercy on him, said that the transferring of human organs to other humans is forbidden in Islam. Perhaps he feared trafficking. But if you set limits, grounds, and laws on the advancement of modern science, the process becomes beneficial to humans and does not contradict religion. In another example, God said,

"And marks, and by the stars guide themselves"[115]

---

[114] Luqman, verse 17.
[115] Al-Nahal, verse 16.

The interpretations of the past say that man was guided during his travels by knowledge of the position of the stars. That is true, but in our time, does an airplane pilot have to know the stars to know his destination and altitude? Our earth is a planet. It is in continuous motion. But it has a magnetic field and gravity like any star. In navigation today, a barometer is influenced by the gravity of the earth to help the pilot gauge his height, and a compass influenced by the earth's magnetism helps the pilot navigate to their destination.

In another example, God said,

"Have they not seen that we come and reduce the Land from its sides?"[116]

Reducing the land may be understood as a rise of sea level. Due to new scientific discoveries, we now know that earth is losing land area to water, such as Tuvalu Islands in the Pacific.

Add to that the distorted and falsely claimed hadiths. Al-Bukhari"[117], may God rest his soul, collected many hadiths of 'Prophet Mohammad, but today I find books of Bukhari's hadiths in varying editions and with additions to suit different Islamic sects! Some of these sects were created after the death of Al-Bukhari!

Today, some people are abandoning Islam because of the incorrect information relayed to them that is falsely attributed to Islam. The information does not answer their questions and does not match reality or logic. Examples include cutting off a thief's hand, hitting one's wife, and many more unrealistic

---

[116] Al Ra'd, verse 41.
[117] Sahih Al-Bukhari, ISBN-13:978-1567445190, Maktba Dar-US-Islam

interpretations of our holy Qur'an. In the thief example, God used an Arabic word that can mean "cutting," but can also mean "keeping his hand away." Similarly, the Arabic word translated "hitting" can also mean "keeping distance between." The person of today differs from his ancestors. He is a materialist who believes in the senses and doubts the unseen. So, to find the correct way to Islam, we must clarify the merits of the Islamic religion for existing life. God created the universe and laid down rules and laws for it to work. He gave us a catalog that shows us how we can live happily. God does not need us, but we need him. God knows everything, and we do not know everything. Many real believers have volunteered to show the right values of Islam, despite opposing minds.

I respect all the hadiths of Prophet Mohammad, but we cannot deduce from them a legal ruling unless this ruling was applied at the time of our noble Messenger and is in line with his teachings, but we should follow hadiths that describe the manners of the Prophet in his behavior with those around him. He was sent to fulfill righteous morality. We have to be careful because transferring speech and information over many years and through several people can lead to confusion. Some words and letters can be forgotten, misrepresented, or diminished, leading to the loss of its original meaning.

In addition, I believe that we cannot deduce from a hadith a new ruling on religion, because the entire rulings of religion are present in the holy Qur'an, and their interpretations are cleared through authentic hadiths.

A hadith based on an action and recorded visually and mentally by a follower of Islam can be remembered. Once it is narrated, it becomes audible. Any hadith that was practically applied, recognized, and had its significance understood (such as prayer techniques, hajj rituals, fasting methodology, and many others) are what we can utilize.

Almighty God said,

> "What the messenger brought to you, take it, and what he forbids you about, so finish."[118]

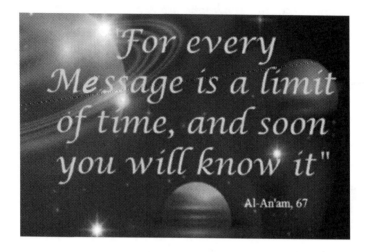

For every Message is a limit of time, and soon you will know it"

Al-An'am, 67

---

[118] Al-hashr, verse 7.

16

PHILOSOPHY OF RECYCLING

God has created various benefits in life stemming from the principle of recycling, God said,

"And there are those who bury gold and silver and spend it not in the way of Allah: announce unto them a most grievous penalty."[119]

It is supposed that gold, silver, and money should not be stockpiled but rather circulated from one man to another. Money is to be used in reviving trade, industry, and agriculture, and in creating profit for those who own it and those who work for it. Money must always be mobile. We increase its value by adding work, so we benefit and pay charity (*zakat*). Money's value is reduced with time. Recycling money through work and trade is a principle imposed by Islam.

God said,

"By no means have you attained righteousness unless you give freely of that which you love."[120]

---

[119] Al-Taobah, verse 34.
[120] Al-Emran, verse 92.

"Whoever comes up with a good deed will have ten times it's like; and whoever comes up with an evil deed will be repaid only with its equivalent—they will not be wronged."[121]

When you pay *zakat* or do a good deed, the benefit will come back to you and you will gain more. You spend, and then you gain, and then you spend, and then you gain. Thus, the benefits are always recycled.

The principle of circulation can also be seen in water. God said,

"Have you not seen how God propels the clouds, then brings them together, then piles them into a heap, and you see rain drops emerging from its midst? How He brings down loads of hail from the sky, striking with it whomever He wills, and diverting it from whomever He wills? The flash of its lightning almost snatches the sight away."[122]

Seawater in its cycle evaporates and becomes a cloud. Then it descends on the mountains as rain. It will flow through valleys, watering the plants and creatures. Water then returns to the sea and cycles again after it has benefited what God created on this earth.

The temperature of lightning in the sky can reach six thousand degrees Celsius as a result of static electricity when clouds rub each other. This high temperature produces nitric

---

[121] Al-Ana'am, verse 160.
[122] Al-Noor, verse 43.

acid from the nitrogen and oxygen in the air, which turns into nitrate fertilizers when it contacts soil. The fertilizer feeds plants, from which green chlorophyll is made. The chlorophyll in turn decomposes and produces nitrogen and oxygen that nourish the air. Plants grow, reproduce, and bear fruit. Then they die and decompose, to become fertilizers.

Many other examples and verses in the Qur'an speak of **the principle of recycling, which is one of the reasons for the continuity of this life we live.**

God created Adam and deposited in his chromosomes Instincts and Clairvoyance, which are passed on from generation to generation. We are born and grow up to pass on our chromosomes to our children before we die. Thus, God created life from the principle of recycling.

The lie or lack of faith that people believe in is that land resources are limited and not sufficient to maintain an increasing population.

Didn't God say,

> "There is no moving creature on earth but its sustenance depends on God. And He knows where it lives and where it rests. Everything is in a Clear Book."[123]

If we consider the principle of recycling, we will see that there is more than enough in the land. God has given us the vision to create. He has given us the strength to perform and apply. There are still a lot of creative ideas, including the principle of recycling. Their exploitation is in our hands. Our

---

[123] Hud, verse 6.

capacity for insight and thought is unlimited. God has set no restrictions or limits on our minds to take from His knowledge. We still need a lot of development in life and work. We must always think about the abundance of resources in the land, look for it, and recycle it.

It is also a principle of recycling that God created opposites in humans and animals so that life can continue. Encounters between two strong creatures end in one killing the other. This allows the weak to live, leading to the weak becoming strong. Thus life continues. God created a whale to eat fish and shrimp. Then the shrimp eat dead whales.

Praise you, my Lord, how great you are.

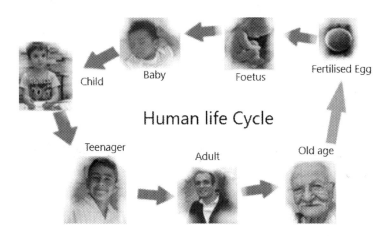

Child   Baby   Foetus   Fertilised Egg

Human life Cycle

Teenager   Adult   Old age

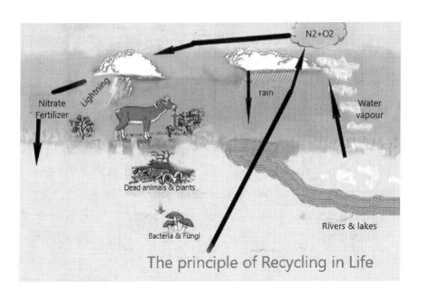

The principle of Recycling in Life

17

NEED, WILL, AND DESIRE

Sometimes we say: This is God's will and desire. But where are man's will and desire?

God has the greatest will, and man represents the smallest wish.

What is the nature of the relationship between man's will and desire? Is it manageable?

Many philosophers and religions have touched on this subject. The pessimistic German philosopher Arthur Schopenhauer"[124] defined desire as being born of needs, deprivation, and suffering. This is the reality of humanity and its essence, since these characteristics are linked to consciousness. Desire is lust accompanied by consciousness. It is self-awareness of what a person wants and seeks through his will. It is the effort that the soul makes to satisfy its desire to preserve itself.

A human will not satisfy all of his desires, because once a desire is satisfied, another is generated. He will constantly search for the realization of the new desire, which means man never rests. Obtaining happiness becomes impossible. That is in the opinion of some philosophers. But

---

[124] Arthur Schopenhauer, The School of Life, Amazon.com

I believe that it is necessary to distinguish between *negative* desire and *positive* desire. People are different. Every human being has definite percentages of these five elements: **intelligence, ambition, potential, endurance,** and **patience.** In addition, he has **personality** components that help him reach his goal. For a person to be successful in reaching what he wishes, and for this wish to be a positive one, *it is essential that the ratios for each of the above-mentioned elements to be positive—that is, above 60 percent.*

- *A positive desire,* when combined with ambition and potential, becomes real. It can be precisely defined, reasonable, and doable. Combined with the right personality, it can lead to success and happiness.

- *A negative desire,* when combined with ambition only, can be called hope. It usually lives in the imagination, undefined, without or with low potential. It is unreasonable, either because of the lack of tools, intelligence, stamina, or character. The person is in constant torment.

Therefore, a person must know his abilities and potential. It is dangerous when Will alone controls the body and the mind to carry out desires. The Will can create false justifications, when the body is used for Will's purposes, the body ages and frays. The Will does not age. It ends with the death of the human.

Some philosophical, Buddhist, and Christian doctrines escape the torment caused by desire by killing desire or even killing oneself. For example, a lover might kill himself if he does not win the love of his beloved. Catholic priests kill the lust for sex by not getting married. So do devout Buddhists.

But Islam does not ask us to kill human desire. Islam rather found a better way to adapt and manage desire within boundaries to create a better life.

God's messenger, Prophet Mohammad said to three Muslims who wanted to live abstinent lives and devote their time to prayer and worship only; "Are you who said so and so? As for me, I fear God more than you, and I am more pious than you, but I fast and break my fast, pray, rest, and marry women, whoever rejects my style is not my follower."

Desires are at numerous levels of need"[125], whether physical, human, or divine. Islam has set the highest standards and rejected destructive and despicable levels. Islam respects the human body and its desires. It considers the body the means to enter paradise or fire. So Islam imposes the satisfaction of the body and its desires from the higher levels of chastity and rejects villainous, destructive levels.

God reminds us in the holy Qur'an that most of the parts of the human body—such as hands, heart, tongue, and skin— will witness on us on the day of resurrection. They are beings connected to our bodies and act on the orders of our minds. The mind is the executive director of the soul in the body. The body's parts are beings, some of which are directly controlled by the human, such as hands, legs, and eyes. Others are controlled involuntarily, yet can still be controlled voluntary by strengthening the will and positive desires through training.

God has created the law of will, i.e., the possibility of controlling our behaviors, actions, and instincts, as well as

---

[125] Mustafa Mahmoud, Will & Desire in Islam, Article, Aug 20, 2018.

some involuntary organs. We can learn to reduce pain and slow down blood circulation.

If we can, with our conscious minds, control our desires, upgrade them, and practice controlling our will, we can make our lives happier. Training exercises to strengthen the will may be difficult. They are like exercises used to strengthen the muscles. These exercises may stress a person psychologically, but the results are good. The results will enable you to reject temptations and harmful pleasures. Here are some examples:

- *Focus on prayer:* In a quiet and secluded place, after saying, "Allahu Akbar," we should leave all thoughts of our world and realize that we are now in presence of our Creator. We are talking to Him and confirming that God is before us, hearing us. Then we may start the first lesson in adjusting our thoughts and our organs. I do it myself and feel the pleasure of focusing. I know it's one of the hardest things to do, because the ideas and distractions of our world pass constantly through our minds. We will get rid of them by focusing and practicing.

- *Fast for Ramadan:* The fast is annual training for refining the desires of the body and the self, such as speech, anger, and sex—because fasting is not only about food.

- *Meditate for twenty minutes a day:* I sit outdoors or indoors in a quiet place, close my eyes, and focus on my breathing (inspiration/exhalation). Concentrating on the breath trains the mind to focus, and these results are amazing.

- *Expel insomnia:* How do you kick thoughts out of your mind to sleep? I lie in my bed and focus my thinking on relaxing my body. First, I relax the big toe of my right foot. Then I go to the index toe and make sure it's relaxed. I take my time. I move on to the middle toe, and then to the fourth toe, and finally to the little toe. Then I repeat the process on my left foot. I work my way up, making sure that each part of my body is relaxed. I take my time. I surely sleep, because I never know where I stopped the exercise.

It is a way to focus your thoughts on one subject.

18

DESIRE AND HABITS

What is a **habit**? A habit is **a behavior we repeat many times**. It is hard to do at first because we need to learn it and convince our perception to do it. Then it becomes easy because our brains like it and consider it axiomatic without requiring unnecessary energy expenditure.

The human brain is a super-developed computer. If we commit to repeating a certain behavior, our brains convert it into a nervous adaptation. Then it becomes a habit, done in an orderly and continuous manner without thought. For example, it's hard for a baby to stand up for the first time. But soon he walks and runs while his thoughts are occupied with something else.

If our brains did not have habits, we wouldn't be able to work, move, and think about many things at the same time.

The energy needed to acquire a habit is usually influenced by effort and internal factors such as will and desire. There are also outside factors, such as one's partner, community, and available time.

Some habits are good and some are bad. Good habits are the ones that create a successful human being. Bad habits destroy him. Unfortunately, it's easy to develop a bad habit because at first you don't need a lot of effort and you see its tempting results immediately. Examples are smoking, drinking alcohol, and negative thinking.

Prophet Mohammad said, "A strong man is not the one who wrestles, but the strong man is he who controls himself when angry."[126]

A good habit initially requires more effort, and results appear after days or weeks Examples include walking, critical thinking, and positive thinking.

Getting rid of a bad habit requires great effort, because to remove it, one needs to avoid the usual culprits. One must have a strong will to ignore one's surroundings and remarks from others. One must not be weak in the face of temptation.

The Messenger of God (pbuh) said, "He who searches for good is given to him, and who protects himself from evil is protected from it." [127]

In other words, habits stem from the Will. Weak Wills cannot control habits, while strong Wills can. The willpower of man helps him organize his life and contributes greatly to his success in study and work"[128]. Willpower can also maintain his health and keep him away from anything harmful.

Will, like a muscle, can improve and strengthen through training. As an example, the will can be built through fasting for the month of Ramadan. Believers stop eating and drinking through the daylight hours and refrain from anger, backbiting, gossip, and complaint. It is one-month of self-training in patience, which God has prescribed to his believers.

---

[126] Sahih Al-Bukhari, ISBN-13:978-1567445190, Maktba Dar-US-Islam
[127] Sahih Al-Bukhari, ISBN-13:978-1567445190, Maktba Dar-US-Islam
[128] Napoleon Hill, Think & Grow Rich, Book, 1937 Edition.

God said,

"O, you who believe! Fasting is prescribed to you as it was prescribed to those before you.... Fasting for a fixed number of days.... And it is better for you that you fast if you only knew."[129]

At an American university in 1972, the marshmallow test was conducted on a group of children whose activities and progress in life were followed for the next twenty years. At first, the children were individually placed in front of pieces of candy and asked not to eat them until they were authorized. They were promised that if they adhered to the instructions, they would be rewarded with another piece of candy. If they ate the marshmallow without waiting, they would not be rewarded with the extra piece. These experiences continued for a while. Years later, researchers found that those who demonstrated the most patience became more successful in their lives.

Prophet Mohammad said: "Fasting is half the patience, fasting the month of patience and three days."[130]

Weak-willed people cannot get rid of bad habits if they have them. They often complain about their miserable condition. Even if their situation is better than others, they become unhappy by self-inspiration. **Thus, when a weak individual hears a negative comment from someone else, he is quickly influenced, because he lacks self-confidence.**

---

[129] Al-Baqara, verse 183, 184.
[130] Sahih Al-Bukhari, ISBN-13:978-1567445190, Maktba Dar-US-Islam.

If you want to destroy the morals of a society, cover vice habits with freedom or relegion

Fahim Jauhary

19

GLANDS ARE BODY INSTRUMENTS

God has forbidden man to eat pork for reasons that only God knows. God said,

> "He has forbidden you carrion, and blood, and the flesh of swine, and anything consecrated to other than God. But if anyone is compelled by necessity, without being deliberate or malicious, then God is Forgiving and Merciful."[131]

If we look at the biological composition of a pig, we find that its hormones are nearly identical to those of humans"[132]. Therefore, drug development companies test their new drugs on pigs"[133] before giving them to humans, to make sure that these drugs are effective.

In the human body, there are more than fifty glands that produce enzymes and hormones. This is called the endocrine system. These glands secrete specific amounts of each hormone. The hormones go into the stomach or into

---

[131] Al-Nahel, verse 115.

[132] *Iowa state Unv, pST, Biotech.*

[133] En.m.wikipedia.org, Pigs are biologicaly similar to humans.

the bloodstream to connect to the area designated for them. Hormones, the body's chemical messengers, are micro-devices that control us. They regulate the management of all activities within the body system: reproduction, growth, disease, and much more. They even affect our activity, moods, and desires. For example, the pepsin enzyme in the stomach breaks protein into peptides. A decrease in the thyroid hormone will cause fatigue and weight increase. The pituitary gland is responsible for human height, weight, and rate of maturation. The lymphatic gland is responsible for resistance to germs. The pineal gland is responsible for changing the psychological state in humans and for regulating time. Sex determination and sexual conditions are controlled by sex hormones such as estrogen, which reigns in the female body. Estrogen also regulates important pathways in Schizophrenia, mitochondrial function, even stress system"[134]. Hermaphroditism is a disease or disturbance in the secretion of sex hormones, or what is called a hormone disorder.

When a hormone disorder is diagnosed, the doctor usually gives the patient a certain hormone in a definite concentration. For example, thyroxin is given in the case of hypothyroidism.

If we eat pork, its hormones, which as I mentioned are similar to human hormones, get transferred into our blood, leading to some of our hormone levels increasing. This can cause an imbalance that affects organs, mood, behavior, and even sexuality. Such diseases can be treated.

---

[134] Prescription treatment website, http://en.m.wikipedia.og.

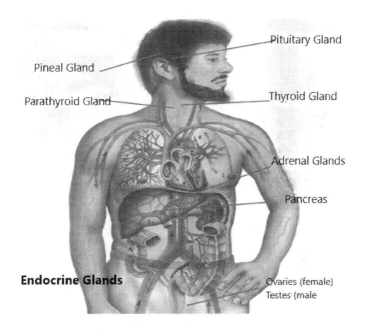

Pineal Gland

Parathyroid Gland

Pituitary Gland

Thyroid Gland

Adrenal Glands

Pancreas

Endocrine Glands

Ovaries (female)
Testes (male

20

CLAY RACE

The Qur'an indicates that God created our father Adam from mire molded clay, which is a mineral compounds plus organic compounds plus water. God said, "Behold! Thy Lord said to the angels:

> "I am about to create man, from mire molded Clay into shape; when I have fashioned him in due proportion, and breathed into him of My spirit, fall you down in obeisance unto him.'"[135]

Mire molded clay is black, dry clay with a sharp scent. Scientifically, it is a mixture of oxides, hydroxides, and mineral salts, such as calcium, phosphorus, and silica. The smell is caused by the presence of organic hydrocarbons.

God also said,

> "Man, we did create from a strain of clay."[136]

God then explains with scientific accuracy how the embryo, which feeds on the mother's blood, is formed. The mother's

---

[135] Alhijr, verses 28–29.
[136] Al-Mo'menoon, verse 12.

blood comes from the food that is originally grown from the clay land. The clay strain consists of different elements. Our Lord left us to research and reflects on it this collection of atoms. Hydrogen has one proton, helium has two protons, and lithium has three protons, and so on. Each element's atomic structure is distinguished from that before it in the periodic table, a series that increases by one proton. The Russian scientist Mendeleev discovered this series and set forth the periodic table of the elements, from which God created everything in our world.

All plants grow from clay. Animals eat plants, and humans eat plants and animals. By the power of God, sperm is formed in the male body. Then it turns into a leech, and then an embryo, then bone, and the bones become coated with flesh. It is born a human, full of spirit and insight in a most beautiful form. That form consists of carbon, hydrogen, nitrogen, calcium, sodium, iron, carbon, and oxygen. Blessed be God; He is the best Creator.

God said,

> "We created the humankind from an essence of clay, then We made him, a drop, in a secure receptacle (the womb), then We created from the drop, a clot (of congealed blood) and We created the clot into bite size tissue, then We created the bite size tissue into bones, then We clothed the bones with flesh, and then produced it other creation. Blessed is Allah, the Best of creators!"[137]

---

[137] Al-M'minoon, verses 12–15.

Thus, God describes his creation to humans in delightful detail, which took man hundreds of years after the Qur'an came down on our Prophet Mohammad (puh) to discover. This undermines the so-called Darwin theory"[138], which claims that all living organisms come from common ancestors, and then differentiate into a tree of d species due to different conditions and environments. But God created man from clay. God also created other creatures, but God did not blow them out of His soul and did not give them the clairvoyance that he gave to humans. God honored man. God created man well. Then God breathed into man from His soul. God made the angels prostrate themselves to man. God gave man insight and has granted him the ability to speak, so He created in his mouth and face forty muscles to speak and to express his opinions and his feelings.

God said,

"Indeed, We created the human with the fairest stature."[139]

"We have honored the children of Adam, and carried them on both land and sea. We have provided them with good things and greatly preferred them above much of Our creation."[140]

God also abolished any mediation between Himself and man.

---

[138] Charles Darwin, The Descent of Man, Book, International bestseller.

[139] Al-Teen, verse 4.

[140] Isra', verse 70.

God said,

"When My worshipers ask you about Me, I am near. I answer the supplication of the suppliant when he calls to Me; therefore, let them respond to Me and let them believe in Me, in order that they will be righteous."[141]

God has honored the human family.

God said,

"Worship Allah and do not associate anything with Him. Be kind to parents and near kinsmen, to the orphans and to the needy, to your neighbor who is your kindred, and to the neighbor at your far side, and the companion at your side, and to the destitute traveler, and to that which your right hands owns. Allah does not love he who is proud and struts."[142]

In many verses, God gave human beings, male and female, the right to decent lives in this world, bestowing on them freedom of thought, equality, honorable presentation, and property safety.

---

[141] Al-Baqara, verse 186.
[142] Al-Nesa', verse 36.

And indeed, We created humankind1 from an extract of clay, then placed each ˹human˺ as a sperm-drop1 in a secure place, then We developed the drop into a clinging clot ˹of blood˺, then developed the clot into a lump ˹of flesh˺, then developed the lump into bones, then clothed the bones with flesh, then We brought it into being as a new creation.1 So Blessed is Allah, the Best of Creators.

Almu'minun (The Believer)
(Verses 12-14)

21

ECONOMY IN LIVING

To rejoice in God's many blessings upon us in this world is a nice thing. From what is permissible, we must enjoy the adornment of life and the goodness of sustenance that God brought to His servants.

God said,

> "Say: Who hath forbidden the beautiful gifts of Allah, which He hath produced for his servants, and the things, clean and pure, which He hath provided for sustenance? Say they are, in the life of this world, for those who believe and purely for them on the Day of Judgment."[143]

One of the worst and ugliest habits is wasting what God has bestowed upon us, such as showing off a suit, dress, or fancy car to make those around us feel inferior. Throwing lavish parties to show off in front of guests under the pretext of honoring them is false generosity. Overeating, overdrinking, over accessorizing, and overdressing are habits that can bring us a range of problems—not only material complications, but also physical, psychological, and social health issues. Excess is the cause of illness, envy, and anger from others.

---

[143] Al-A'araf, verse 32.

Ramadan separates manifestations of generosity and the scourge of extravagance, which is denied in the holy Qur'an about twenty-three times. God Almighty forbids us from extravagance in his grace.

God said:

> "But waste not by excess: for Allah loves not the wasters."[144]

> "Eat and drink: But waste not by excess, for Allah, loves not the wasters."[145]

> "And the Transgressors will be Companions of the fire!"[146]

> "And follow not the bidding of those who are extravagant. Who make mischief in the land, and mend not their ways?"[147]

> "Those who, when they spend, are not extravagant and not niggardly, but hold a just balance between those extremes."[148]

Ramadan is not a month of wasting and delving in the pleasures of food. Ramadan fasting is a healthy, educational and social school, based on patience, self-violation, breaking

---

[144] Al-Ana'am, verse 141.
[145] Al-A'raf, verse 31.
[146] Ghafer, verse 43.
[147] Alshua'ara, verses 151–152.
[148] Alfurqan, verse 67.

lust and respect for order, commitment of community and charity to the poor, sympathy for the poor and needy, and cleansing of the soul. **It is a month of giving to the poor, a month of patience to strengthen the will of a Muslim.**

22

SLAVERY AND RELIGION

Throughout the ages, the sources of slavery have been and continue to be many. The Qur'an has been calling for **equality, liberty** and **human rights** for more than one thousand four hundred years. Its principles call for **justice** and **equality** among human beings, and these principles are incompatible with having another human being as a slave. What is permissible is slavery for God alone or the worship of God; this is what it means to be Muslim for God.

But one of the principles accepted by people in ages past was that prisoners of war could be exploited as slaves. So God put in his Qur'an many guidance for freeing prisoners and slaves.

The honorable Prophet Mohammad came to complete morality, not to produce a revolution that would be rejected by the Arabs that time, those who had a lot of slaves. Firstly, he prescribed to the captive that if he became a Muslim or taught a Muslim how to write, he could go free. That was meant to stop bloodshed and create respect for the captured as a human being. God decreed that regardless of a prisoner's religion, we must feed him from what we eat and give him clothing from what we wear until the war ends.

Islam legalized emancipation and did not legalize slavery. It prescribed for each penance the liberation of a slave. Whoever had a maid slave and did not wish to free her was allowed to marry her, so that she would be entitled to her full rights as a wife.

It was therefore assumed that after a generation of Muslims, there would be no bondage among human beings.

God said:

> "O mankind! We created you from a single pair of a male and a female, and made you into nations and tribes, that you may know each other. Verily the most honored of you in the sight of Allah, he who is the most righteous of you, and Allah has full knowledge and is well acquainted."[149]

> "But he has not broken through the difficult pass. And what can make you know what is (breaking through) the difficult pass? It is freeing of a slave."[150]

Unfortunately, some of those who claimed to be religious did not understand this logic. Slavery continued even 1,300 years after the descent of the heavenly message. Some examples include a slave market in Yemen during the thirteenth century. The trafficking of slaves in Yemen and surrounding areas continued into the nineteenth century. We find in the notes of

---

[149] Alhujurat, verse 13.
[150] Albalad, verses 11–13.

the traveler Ibn Khaldun"[151] that whenever he passed through a Muslim country, the sultan would grant him a maid to enjoy and leave. During the reign of Hammoud ibn Muhammad, sultan of Zanzibar (1896–1902), who claimed Islam, there was human trafficking until he complied with the British colonizers' demands to prohibit it. What type of Islam is that?

Human freedom came from the Qur'an 1,450 years ago, but today in the age of atoms and world civilization, slavery has evolved in countries around the world. It has become a kind of business, sometimes with legal licenses. Consider job bondage, such as the sale of football players via contracts. There is also the bondage of usury, whereby a country or society is flooded with debt and becomes beholden to creditors. The bondage of thought allows the enslavement of another human being by controlling or forbidding certain ideas.

God said,

> "O people! We created you from a male and a
> female, and made you races and tribes, that
> you may know one another. The best among
> you in the sight of God is the most righteous.
> God is All-Knowing, Well-Experienced."[152]

Prophet Mohammad said, "People are equal like the teeth of a comb."[153]

---

[151] Ibn Khaldun, The Muqaddimah, The Classic Islamic History, Book, Kindle.

[152] Al-Hujurat, verse 13.

[153] Sahih Al-Bukhari, ISBN-13:978-1567445190, Maktba Dar-US-Islam.

23

EARTH SWERVES AND WEATHER CHANGES

The following Quranic verses surprised me, in the name of God, the most gracious and most merciful:

> "Do not the unbelievers see that the heavens and the earth were joined together as one unit of creation before We clove them asunder? We made from water every living thing; will they not then believe? And We have set on the earth mountains standing firm, lest it should shake with them, and We have made therein broad highways for them to pass through: that they may receive guidance. And We have made the heavens as a canopy well-guarded: yet do they turn away from the signs which these things. It is He Who created the Night and the Day, and the sun and the moon: all swim along, each in its Orbital."[154]

Hallelujah, here are five scientific miracles in ten lines. This leads us to scientific thoughts and opinions in these verses.

---

[154] Al-Anbyaa', verses 31–33.

The Heavens

The explosion of the great universe and the creation of the earth mean that the whole universe was bound like a fist and then extended by God to become the earth, planets, and stars. It is still expanding. God said,

"And We constructed the universe with power, and We are expanding it."[155]

Based on previous scientific theories and research from Einstein, Newton, Kepler, and the modern Palmer Laboratories"[156],[157], we know that the diameter of the universe is 93 billion light-years and still expanding because of **centrifugal forces**. The location of each celestial object depends on its mass and the speed of its rotation. But mass decreases with time and leads to a reduction in the speed of rotation. This weakens the strength of the centrifugal force.

God goes on to tell us about the end of this universe and to assure us of His oneness:

"To Allah do belongs the unseen of the heavens and the earth, and to Him goes back every affair."[158]

---

[155] Al-Dhariyat, verse 47.
[156] PJE Palmer, The Gravitational Instability of the Universe, NASA 1967.
[157] Stephen Hawking, A Brief History of Time, Audio Book, Google Play.
[158] Hood, verse 123.

That is, this universe, which is of God's command, will eventually return to God and disappear.

In another verse, God explains how heaven and the planets will turn to Him. There will be **attractive forces** between the planets and stars. The influence of centrifugal forces will end or subside. Gravity will become very powerful, attracting everything—even the light. God tells us that the universe will return as its first beginning:

> "The Day that we roll up the heavens like a scroll rolled up for books, even as We produced the first creation, so shall We produce a new one: a promise We have undertaken: truly shall We fulfill it."[159]

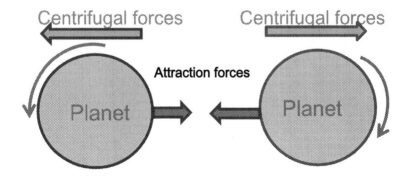

---

159 Al-Anbyaa', verse 104.

The Water

Biologists disagree"[160] about where the living cell originated. But most scientists, based on fossil microbial research, believe that life began in the water 3.5 billion years ago, millions of years before God created our father Adam. Water in oceans is created for the durability of life. Without water, the sun's heat would raise earth's temperature and burn what is on earth in an instant. The specific heat of water is much higher than that of rocks and solid material. Seawater stores heat from the sun in the daytime without getting hot, and releases that heat at night.

Besides that, seawater evaporates to become clouds, and clouds rub each other to release high-voltage static electricity, which produces lightning. Lightning converts oxygen and nitrogen from the air into nitrates that dissolves in rainwater. Rainwater falls to the ground, and the nitrates fertilize plants, creating life on earth.

Earth Shaking

Check God's words: "And We have set on the earth mountains standing firm, lest it should shake with them." This means that God constantly and very accurately keeps earth balanced so as not to sway or shake and cause the deaths of its inhabitants. Imagine that your car's car wheel is unbalanced and you drive at a speed of 50 kilometers per hour. What will happen to the car? Of course the car will shake. The faster you go, the more you annoy your passengers. Earth rotates at a rate of 1,660 kilometers per hour (If we divide earth's

---

[160] Michael Marshall, The Secret of how life on earth Began, Book, Amazon.

circumference by the hours of the day, we get: = 40000/24), or three times faster than an airplane. But we, its inhabitants, do not feel any vibration because God continuously adjusts earth's balance so it does not shake.

The reason for recent changes in earth's climate is not only the carbon dioxide emitted by factories and cars—known as the formation of the so-called greenhouse effect that heats earth's surface—but also the melting of huge mountains of snow at earth's poles. Mountains of snow have disappeared from their position. What is the result?

> The centers of the poles have shifted to maintain earth's balance"[161]. That is, earth's axis of rotation has shifted its orbit little by little. Spring now overlaps with summer, summer overlaps with winter, and winter overlaps with spring. Another theory about the shifting of earth's poles is that a huge, molten iron mass in the center of earth moves slowly every few years, shifting earth's magnetic field back and forth.

> Let's also think about the water from that melted snow. Where does it go? Of course, to the sea, and therefore raises the sea level a few millimeters every year or more. Eventually, the water will cover parts of the land. Consider what God Almighty said:

"See they not that We gradually reduce the land from its outlying borders?"[162]

---

[161] National Geografic, North Pole Displacement, 2016/04.

[162] Al-Ra'ad, verse 41.

Canopy Heavens

Our Lord reminds us that the sky preserves the earth, or rather is a keeper of earth and those on it:

"And We have made the heavens as a canopy well-guarded." How?

Earth is a massive magnet, and the magnetic field around it in the sky saves it from the deadly X and gamma rays emitted by the sun.

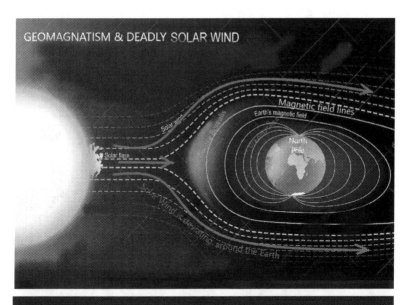

GEOMAGNATISM & DEADLY SOLAR WIND

Magnetic field lines
Earth's magnetic field
Solar wind
Solar flare
North pole
Solar Wind is deviating around the Earth

What happens when a CME hits Earth?
1. Solar wind is deflected around Earth
2. Deflected solar wind drags Earth's magnetic field with it
3. Magnetic field lines "reconnect" and accelerate particles
4. Accelerated particles follow field lines to Earth
Aurora is produced when particles hit Earth's atmosphere

Planet Orbits

The sun, moon, and earth rotate, each in its orbit, and do not interfere with each other. The word "swimming" in the Quranic verse means that they move because of the forces of their own, from within them. Our ancestors thought that earth was flat and the sun and moon moved in a circle around it. We now know that earth is round, or oval shape as it is described by God:

> "And the earth after that He Da'haha (=spread it like an Ostrich egg)"[163]

---

[163] Al-Nazi'at, verse 30

24

PHARAOHS MADE CEMENT

When I went for hajj in 2011, I was reading the Qur'an in an Arafat tent. Young Iraqis sat down near me and said, "Increase our knowledge, O Sheikh." (I was bearded.)

I said, "I am neither a sheikh nor a scholar of religion, but come and let us meditate with some verses from the Qur'an."

"I opened the Qur'an and read, "Then ignite for me, O, Haman! (A fire) on the clay and build for me a tower that I may look at the God of Moses. And I do think he is among the liars."[164]

Since I am a chemical engineer, I remembered:

- The Romans built their houses and castles, which still exist, from volcanic ashes.
- Carbonates of calcium, iron, magnesium, aluminum, and chromium, when heated above the temperature of one thousand degrees Celsius, lose carbon dioxide and turn into oxides.
- When mixing those oxides with water and placing them in molds, the lost carbon dioxide is restored over

---

[164] Al-qasas, verse 38.

time from the water and atmosphere, and the molded material returns to its origin as stone, i.e., cement.

- The word "ignite" in the Quranic verse does not mean "heat up." It means to make fire at a temperature over one thousand degrees Celsius.
- This is how factories manufacture cement.
- The pyramid's stones do not contain fossils or veins; though volcanic stones, they are not from quarries or volcanic rocks.

That means that the pharaoh of Egypt was asking the architect of the building, Haman, to light a fire under the clay stones, turn them into oxides, and make construction cement, just as we do today. So simply, God tells us how the pharaohs built the pyramids.

Old Quick lime production Plant

25

EMPTY COSMIC VOIDS

Theories about the universe are either disproven, found to be unsubstantiated, or declared to be "very likely." Things that scientists believe to be true can be undone by new discoveries.

Recent discoveries prove that galactic structures are connected by **dark matter**. Dark matter is a hypothetical substance that cosmologists believe holds structures like galaxies together. The idea is that there must be something that keeps galaxies from flying apart. It's dark, and thus unseen, because it doesn't interact with electromagnetic radiation (light).

When man launched a manned rocket to the moon, he found that the space between the earth and the moon is dark, even though the sun is shining.

The Creator, in the Qur'an, mocks those who do not believe in him and says: If we open a door for them to ascend to heaven and come out of the atmospheric layer, they will not see anything and say, Our eyes are blinded, or we are enchanted:

"Even if We opened for them a gateway into the sky, and they began to ascend through it. They would still say, "Our eyes are hallucinating; in fact, we are people bewitched."[165]

This verse gives us these facts:

- In the sky between stars and planets, there is a great void.
- The light penetrates the void and does not illuminate it because there is no substance to reflect on it.
- Light does not come out of the eye, but enters it.

God also tells us about the bonds around planets; the planets are woven together. God swears by the woven sky and addressing our master Prophet:

> "What you are promised is true. Judgment will take place. By the sky that is woven."[166]

A team of astronomers"[167], using the Baryon Oscillation Spectroscopic Survey, discovered great wall filaments. The universe resembles a cosmic web of matter surrounding empty voids—and these walls are the thickest threads. A group of scientists at Princeton University also discovered this filament. The clusters may not be bound by gravity, and it is possible they will never be.

---

[165] Al-Tdariyat, verses 5–7.
[166] Al-Hijr, verses 14–15.
[167] Astronomy & Astrophysics, Volume 588, id.L4, 4 pp.

>>>> Done with God's help<<<<

REFERENCES

- Adam Grant, How to think like a wise Person, Syndicated from linkedin, Nov 20, 2013.
- Adnan Al-Rifai, The Great Miracle, Wikipedia.
- Ali Bin Abu-Talib, from a poem, Facebook.
- Al-Jalalayn, Tafsir, Book by Al-Mahalli & Al-Suyuti, i.e Al-gashiah, verse 20.
- Arthur Schopenhauer, The School of Life, Amazon.com.
- Astronomy & Astrophysics, Volume 588, id.L4, 4 pp.
- Bertrand Russell, The history of western Philosophy, Book published by Simon & Schuster, NY.
- Binbaz.org.sa/fatwas.
- Brian Tracy, Proven Process for Success, Audio Book, Amazon.
- Bihar Al-Anwar, V.14, P.317,No 17
- Bertrand Russell, The history of western Philosophy, Book published by Simon & Schuster, NY.
- Confucius, Famous Quotes About life, Amazon.
- Charles Darwin, The Descent of Man, Book, International bestseller.
- Duncan MacDougall, Scientific Study published in 1907, Massachusetts.
- En.m.wikipedia.org, Pigs are biologicaly similar to humans.
- Georg W. F. Hegel, Most Famous Quotes about life.
- Igor Grossman, Wisdom Bias & Balance, Journal Article 2018 Dec., Waterloo Univ.Canada.
- Iben Roshd, History of Islam Philosophers, Hindawi.org/ Books.

- Iowa state Unv, pST, Biotech.
- Ibn Khaldun, The Muqaddimah, The Classic Islamic History, Book, Kindle.
- Igor Grossman, Wisdom Bias & Balance, Journal Article 2018 Dec., Waterloo Univ.Canada.
- Joseph Murphy, The power of your subconscious Mind, Book, 1981, Amazon, CA, USA.
- John Assaraf, How I bought my dream House, You Tube Video, Apr. 6,2016
- Mohammad Shahroor, Book, the Qur'an & the Book, Amazon.
- Marcus E.R. & Debra A.Gusnard, Appraising the Brain's Energy Budget, Pdf, July 29, 2002.
- Marc Bekoff, Animal Instincts, Berkeley, edu./Mar 08,2011
- Mitwalli Sha'rawi, Celestical science & Cosmic science, YouTube.
- M.M. Al-Sha'rawi, Fate & Predestination, Book, Kindle
- Mohammad Shodab, Zamzam Water, Prophet Honest talks, Mar 28, 2019
- Michael Marshall, The Secret of how life on earth Began, Book, Amazon.
- Mustafa Mahmoud, Will & Desire in Islam, Article, Aug 20, 2018.
- N. Swaminathan, Why does Brain Need so much Power, Pdf, April 29, 2008.
- Napoleon Hill, Think & Grow Rich, Book, 1937 Edition.
- National Geographic, North Pole Displacement, 2016/04.
- Philip K. Dick, How to build a Universe, The Marginalian, 1972
- Prescription treatment website, http://en.m.wikipedia.og.
- PJE Palmer, The Gravitational Instability of the Universe, NASA 1967.

- Ralph W. Emerson, Brainy Quotes, Facebook.
- Steven J. Stein, Emotional Intelligence, E. Book, M. D., 2011.
- Saul McLeod, Sigmund Freud's Theories, Article 2018
- Sahih Al-Bukhari, ISBN-13:978-1567445190, Maktba Dar-US-Islam
- Stephen Hawking, A Brief History of Time, Audio Book, Google Play.
- Stephen S. Hall, From Philosophy to Neuroscience, Book, Amazon.
- S.Ryan, Wisdom, Stanford Encyclopedia of Philosophy/ Spring 2007 ed.
- The Trials of Socrates, famous-trials.com.

Printed in the United States
by Baker & Taylor Publisher Services